He's My Daughter

A Mother's Journey

He's My Daughter

A Mother's Journey to Acceptance

Lynda Langley

Indra Publishing

Indra Publishing
PO Box 7, Briar Hill, Victoria, 3088, Australia.

© Lynda Langley 2002
Typeset in Palatino by Fire Ink Press.
Made and Printed in Australia by McPherson's Printing Group.

National Library of Australia Cataloguing-in-Publication data:

Langley, Lynda, 1945–.
He's my daughter: a mother's journey to acceptance

ISBN 0 9578735 5 7

1. Langley, Lynda, 1945–. 2. Mothers – Biography. 3. Transsexuals – Biography. 4. Sex change. 5. Mother and child. I. Title.

305.9066

Contents

Sometime in your life you will go on a journey.
It will be the longest journey you have ever taken ...

Katherine Sharp

To all the other mothers

Introduction

Many books have been written about transsexuals. There are scientific screeds complete with full colour plates of surgery with graphic detail, volumes of research, biographies about transsexuals and autobiographies written by transsexuals.

I am the mother of a transsexual. This is my story. It is written entirely from my own perspective. It's about how I see things and understand transsexuality. If any facts are wrong, well that is where my education about the subject needs more study and time. But at this time in my life, this is how it is for me.

As well as my frantic quest for information and education, I desperately needed to know how other mothers felt, how they coped with their feelings and how they related to their transsexual son or daughter.

I found very little on the subject of a mother's experience, except one short article on the internet and others by professionals who reported about mothers' feelings. That's all. There may be more that has been written, but I haven't come across anything as yet. I have also met the mother of a female to male transsexual and briefly, a mother who has a male to female, son/daughter.

Where are the other mothers? Maybe if I tell my story, others will follow, or listen and know they are not alone. I need to know I am not alone.

In my story, names have been changed or omitted altogether as I wish to protect the innocence of the children in my family and I want their privacy guarded until they are an age where they can make their own choices on these matters. My hope is they will be broad-minded, tolerant, loving and loyal in their relationships and that they will have learnt that all humanity is valuable, no matter how different a person may be, even when that person is your parent or relative.

There will be no sensational photographs used in this book. The readers will have to imagine for themselves how Tony looks now and how he looked before. If they are curious they might look at themselves, for one way or another, more or less, we are all partly male and partly female.

Prologue

"It's a boy," the nurse proclaimed.

Between my white-stockinged and stirruped legs was a view of Dr. Prasad's dark-chocolate coloured face. He held aloft a black-haired newborn, confirming what I'd heard. I had definitely given birth to a well-endowed boy baby.

As I recall my son's birth I wonder what kind of witch-doctor Dr. Prasad was. What sort of voodoo was performed on my baby on that warm summer night, almost thirty-five years ago? I remember the moment of Tony's birth was a mere forty-five minutes past the witching hour.

The white clock on the wall of the labour ward matched the sterile environment. No wonder the doctor's black face was in such stark contrast to the surreal surroundings in which I had given birth.

Utter nonsense, I tell myself. Of course the doctor was not some weird magician muttering spells over my baby son. Yet when a mother can find no scientific answer and unusually painful emotions are involved, illogical thoughts intrude. Such was the depth of my distress when I heard of my firstborn's dilemma.

Many times over those initial weeks, as I attempted to understand why, I relived Tony's birth and his childhood. I went back to it over and over. I saw my baby. I felt his soft dark hair. I smelt his newborn scent and the soft aroma of a talc-bottomed, freshly bathed toddler. I recall the sweaty skin of a five-year-old as he ran breathless to show me a new found treasure with special markings – a leaf fossil beautifully pressed into an ancient grey rock. I gave that stone to Tony's daughter. I hope she keeps it forever.

Searching for clues, combing through memories, I blamed myself. I blamed God. I just didn't understand why. How could nature play such a cruel trick on my son? Yet if all of the world's psychiatrists, scientists, counsellors, doctors, researchers and physicians cannot agree on an explanation, then reasoned thought tells me there is no way I can know why either. But none of those professionals are my son's mother. I am his mother and I needed to know why.

After months of fruitless soul-searching, days of grief, and countless hours of tears, I came to a see-sawing conclusion; some days I accepted things, other days I refused to acknowledge reality.

Nature somehow went askew. No tears of frustration, no weeping mother-love, no feeling sorry for myself and for my son can change what is. Facts are facts. I could go under, drown in my own tears or I could swim to the surface and survive.

In my head I was saying, "My son is a woman. There, I have said it. He has been trapped in his male body long enough. Let him be free. He is my daughter."

The trouble was my heart had not yet followed my head. There was much that I yet had to come to grips with.

1

Wednesday Evening, 23 July 1997

Something extraordinary occurred and it took place on a misty, dark evening when my mind and heart were already filled to the brim with emotion.

It was 6.15 p.m. and a telephone call from the other side of Australia, more than 3000 kilometres away may as well have been transmitted via the moon. The message was alien.

When the telephone rang we had just sat down to dinner. The food in our mouths was somehow swallowed, but we left the rest of the meal on our plates. I knew as soon as my husband, Richard, took the call that something bad had happened. His face drained to ashen. He pulled his chair closer to the phone and sat with a shocked look that began to cause his skin to redden upward from his chin, stopping at his eyebrows. The rest of his face remained white.

I can't remember much of what I heard of that conversation. It has disappeared without trace. I knew something serious had happened to our eldest son, Tony. It was his wife on the phone, ringing from their interstate home; I'd gleaned that much. I recall single words, like hospital, surgery, blood and transfusion.

The telephone wasn't even returned to its cradle before I demanded to know what was wrong. What had happened to Tony? Why was he in hospital? Richard had no way to find the right words to tell me gently.

Richard said, "Tony's cut himself," concealing part of the news.

"Where?" I demanded to know. "He's cut his testicles." I think I said things like, "Oh my God. No. No." I'm not sure. I remember that we all cried a lot.

Within a couple of hours Richard explained the full extent of Tony's injuries.

He had totally castrated himself. He had lost a lot of blood and was in surgery.

2

At 7.00 a.m. that morning Richard pushed the bedclothes back and tumbled out of bed with less than his usual good humour. His whistling, which in the early morning often annoyed me, was missing. He hopped back under the covers, stretched his freckly arm around me and pulled me close. "Don't worry so much, love. It'll be all right." Yet I could tell by the furrow pulled up across his brow, which was usually wrinkle-free, that his words belied his feelings.

We talked for a few minutes, wishing tomorrow's court case was over. Our youngest son, Andrew, was due to face charges for the cultivation and use of marijuana. A jail term was a distinct possibility. The law states that you only get one good behaviour bond ever, and Andrew had used his chance several years earlier, when convicted on a similar charge. This time Andrew had grown quite a crop in various areas of the rented property he shared with his cousins.

Our son had developed a serious addiction to marijuana. He was ill; thin, gaunt, hollow-eyed and breathing wheezily through a severe chest infection when he'd returned home, petrified, lonely and worried about his court case. Consequences had finally caught up with him. He wanted to change, to kick his habit.

Anyone who dismisses marijuana as a soft recreational type of drug, hasn't come into contact with someone addicted to today's 'skunk', a weed many times stronger than previously grown plants; a genetically cultivated nightmare for those people who can't stop using the bong. Its effects can create a person who craves their drug of choice – a person who becomes like someone else. As with any type of substance abuse the user develops a tolerance and requires more and more doses to achieve their desired effect. Behavioural problems emerge, financial worries develop, health deteriorates and the motivation to do anything other than use drugs disappears. Life is a merry-go-round and often it is a ride in which family climb aboard alongside the user. My husband and I hopped on the little horses and paid for the ride with emotional stress, anger, guilt, fear, frustration and grief. Eventually it became a matter of saving our own sanity. There was nothing we could do for Andrew but love him.

We began to say 'No'. It was extremely hard to do at first. We had become so entrenched in what we thought was our duty of care as parents. We took a long time to detach and extricate ourselves from his problem.

Going over all this, and more, Richard and I discussed the next day's court appearance. I'd never been inside a courtroom before. I was terrified. I had no idea what to expect and more than anything dreaded the outcome although I understood that whatever punishment the court meted out to Andrew he would have to accept.

I helped Andrew by taking him to legal aid. That was as far as we were now prepared to go in helping him. We refused to pay for a solicitor or for any fines. At last we realised that these were Andrew's responsibilities, not ours.

A loud ring from the telephone on Richard's side of the bed pulled us back to the moment. A quick glimpse over Richard's shoulder and my brain registered the digital redness at 7.15 a.m. Andrew's legal aid solicitor had rung with urgent news for him. There had been an error in the date of his hearing. It was today – not tomorrow.

No time for slow rising, as was my usual routine. I leapt

out of bed, showered, dressed and prepared tea and toast for the family. Scraping a thin layer of Vegemite onto a slice, I forced myself to eat. I offered some to Andrew, but he was too nervous to take a bite.

Over the past couple of weeks Andrew had been de-toxing in our home. Since the day he'd arrived on our doorstep seeking help, we had been through a rough time together. He came to us a very sick young man, asking to stay. We took him back home, on condition that he seek professional medical help to de-tox. If he was willing to do that, we'd be there for him.

The morning after he arrived, some two weeks earlier, we managed to secure an appointment with a doctor at a drug and alcohol rehabilitation centre. We were glad Andrew took this step, but held no false expectations. He would get well if he really was committed to recovery.

During the time prior to Andrew's appearance in court, I realised that I had a prejudice, perhaps because of the cost factor, I'm not sure. I felt a legal aid solicitor would be a very poor ally in a court case. A person provided by the government to help those less fortunate seemed to me more to do with looking as if justice was being done than actually being of great service to their client. I couldn't have been more wrong.

We arrived at the local courtrooms early. The fine rain had eased. It was cold and clear and the sky had a soft dullness typical of a Melbourne winter day. I shivered with nervous apprehension as I sat between Andrew and Richard attempting small talk while waiting to see the solicitor.

She called the three of us in to a small, austere office. Immediately I warmed to her charming but businesslike manner. A constant worried expression in her eyes hinted at a large work-load. After asking Andrew a few preliminary questions, she began making copious notes on a pad in a large scrawled script. She listened to our story of Andrew's efforts to de-tox, his counselling and his wish to recover.

I think she believed what we told her and she seemed to have faith in Andrew.

Within fifteen minutes she'd prepared a case for Andrew. Prior to his appearance in the courtroom she warned Andrew of the possibility of a jail term, due to the large number of plants that had been confiscated by police. "It would appear too many for one person's use," she said, which might suggest to a cynical magistrate the possibility of dealing. There were no charges to that effect. Nevertheless, it didn't look good. On the plus side, however, Andrew had a letter from his counsellor, proof of his on-going appointments for treatment at the drug and alcohol centre and his own hand-written plea to the court, apologising for what he had done and stressing his wish to reform.

On entering the courtroom we tilted our head forward slightly, as we'd been instructed, showing respect to the magistrate. My knees were trembling. I sat along the bench, a little apart from Andrew, so that he couldn't feel me shaking. He was probably too concerned with his own fears to notice mine, but I didn't wish to make him feel any worse than he already did.

Three cases before us were heard, then our solicitor motioned us forward. She had instructed Andrew to sit in full view of the magistrate, with Richard and I behind and slightly to his right. She wanted to make it clear that Andrew had parental support but was on his own in accepting the consequences of his actions.

The charges were read; then it was the solicitor's turn. She presented Andrew's case clearly, succinctly and with what I thought sounded like just the right amount of pleading on his behalf. She assured the magistrate of Andrew's wish to recover and asked that he not be given a jail sentence, or any fine that could be converted to a community-based order. With a work order came the possibility of Andrew being forced into the company of other offenders. She assured the magistrate of Andrew's parental support, and the fact that he was being supervised in his recovery; that in fact he had not been out of our sight in the past two weeks.

For a moment the magistrate peered at Andrew over the top of his brown-rimmed spectacles. He read all the reports and consulted his computer. For what seemed like an age, he considered his verdict. In the three cases we had witnessed before Andrew's, the magistrate had delivered his sentence quickly. This was not so with Andrew's case. I held my breath hardly daring to breathe lest my heart jump out of its cavity. My son risked imprisonment. I didn't allow myself to dwell on that thought. I stayed in limbo for those minutes, just waiting for the magistrate to make up his mind.

When he finally rose the magistrate spoke quietly and quickly. He gave Andrew the unusual chance of another twelve-month period where he must be of good behaviour and he was ordered to continue treatment for his addiction and to pay $500 to the poor box.

Relief that my son was being given another chance and would not go to jail, washed a warm glow through my body. I cried. Andrew cried. Richard cried. We hugged one another, and smiled as though our faces were constructed from rubber.

We wanted to share the good news with my mother. She lives with us, but was seriously ill in hospital. One of her lungs was partially collapsed. She had pneumonia and a lung infection – pseudomonas, an opportunistic type of infection which attacks those who are frail, elderly or immune suppressed. Sometimes AIDS patients suffer this infection. Her lungs are severely damaged by asthma, and a long period of treatment with steroid drugs has left her susceptible to these sorts of illnesses. She needed something to cheer her. We were too excited by Andrew's reprieve to go home so we drove straight to the hospital.

As we walked the long, sterile corridor on the way to Mum's hospital ward, Andrew noticed a beautiful chapel. I commented that he must have had a guardian angel in court with him. We glanced at the light streaming through the multi-coloured stained glass window as we hurried by, noting its beauty but not knowing the window would come to mean so much to us.

By the time we returned home we all felt exhausted and glad the day was almost over, though happy and relieved at the outcome. Andrew had a long way to go with his recovery, but at least he had another chance and the opportunity to continue treatment, which I felt sure he was unlikely to receive in jail.

We sat down hoping for a quiet dinner together, unaware that our meal would soon be disturbed by an interstate telephone call that changed our lives forever.

3

The Shocking News

It is a long time ago since the phone call that changed my life forever. A great deal of adjustment and acceptance of Toni has taken place over that period. My mind tells me, as well as the psychological treatment that I have undertaken, that events have power to hurt you only if you allow them to. The mind is powerful and I have managed to train it to an extent, yet how come the pit of my stomach still recoils when I remember the first twenty-four hours of that awful time – what I am able to remember that is. Much of that day is a blur. Yet I do recall vividly my second son, Paul's, telephone call when he told me what he felt I must know to be fully prepared for my flight to Perth.

Perhaps if I retell this painful part of my story, it will be possible for me to put it to rest, at least to some extent. We are a large extended family. Richard is one of nine children; I am one of four. Good times and bad are shared. We are there for one another. Although there have been divisions over the past few years the old adage has proven true – 'Blood is thicker than water.' And when there is great trauma we are together, well, almost all of us – but that's another story again.

When Richard put the phone down from Judith's phone call he looked ill. I mean truly ill. I almost thought he was going to pass out and perhaps he almost did. I've never actually asked him to recall his feelings of that time. It's not something we've been able to discuss. How could we? I can barely think about how I felt myself.

"Richard, tell me quick. What's happened? Is Tony all right?"

I knew in my heart that something dreadful had happened. He didn't need to tell me that. But what, I thought – no I don't think I thought at all. Oh I can't really remember; it was all such a blur of disastrous fear.

Richard managed to tell me that Tony had cut his testicles. That didn't seem to make much sense to me. I'd known for about three weeks that Tony had feelings of being female. But I couldn't seem to make that idea sink in – it was all so unreal. What I needed to know now was if he was going to be all right, and how serious was his condition? Richard said he had lost a lot of blood and that Tony was in the operating theatre. They were trying to save his life and trying to repair the damage.

The first thing we did was ring around the family and tell them about the terrible news. I made a few calls and Richard made a few. Much of that night was spent on the telephone. We rang the hospital a couple of times, but no further information about Tony's condition was forthcoming. We were told to ring again later.

When we tried to sleep, only further floods of tears came. This was something too awful to contemplate. In the depth of that long night, I was in the dark. I hadn't been told exactly what had happened. Richard knew. I am not sure if he wanted to protect me or he was unable to say the words, perhaps both. Somehow I managed to prompt him with a few of the right questions and was finally able to work out for myself what had happened. I had to ask direct questions. Richard answered explaining everything that he knew about Tony's castration.

Yet still I didn't know just what 'castration' really meant. Had he cut off his testicles, scrotum and his penis? Could he live without them? Would he die? Was he mad? Was he suicidal?

Somehow, it became my second son, Paul's, duty to tell me exactly what had happened. He gently but firmly explained that Tony had cut out his testicles. He had actually performed an extremely delicate operation on himself without the aid of anaesthetic apart from whisky, or any medical equipment other than a scalpel. Paul explained this type of operation, when it is performed by a surgeon, is known as an orchidectomy. He went on to tell me that Tony had used rubber bands as tourniquets. His penis and most of the scrotum skin was intact. While I listened to Paul, although I did not understand at that time, we would later discover that even in Tony's distressed state, he must have known that he would need some of those parts of his anatomy when he eventually underwent gender reassignment surgery.

I remember begging my son, "Please Paul, don't tell me. I don't want to know what he did or how he did it." But he continued to tell me all of the gory details.

"Mum, you need to know. I have to tell you. You're travelling interstate to the hospital without Dad. You have to be prepared before you get there."

Paul does not know how grateful I am that I went prepared, that I already knew the horrible things that had happened prior to my arrival. I even found out that Tony had discovered how to perform the surgery from the internet. How difficult it must have been for Paul to have to tell his mother those gruesome details.

The bathroom tiles looked dirty. What a silly thing to notice. My head was hanging over the bowl. I'd been sick. I stayed on the floor for a long time. My mind refused to accept what Paul had told me, but I knew the facts were true. My stomach churned and the emptiness caused me to heave again. There was no such restriction on my tears. When do they dry, I wondered?

4

Hospital

From the eighth floor, through the double glass ward window, I could see the beautiful Swan River in the distance. Today the sky was dull and the water looked grey.

As I stared blankly at the view, a scene from an old movie re-wound in my head. I remembered the dark, handsome star talking to his leading lady. "There's always someone in worse pain than you," he advised. She nodded, gave a gentle smile in reply and said, "I know."

At that moment I turned and watched my son, his black hair receding and damp against his yellow/white skin. His eyes were downcast. When he looked at me I saw the depth of his pain, and knew the film star was accurate in his assessment.

Tony sobbed as I held him close. "I'm sorry Mum, I'm sorry." Patting him as if he were a baby again, I hushed him. "It's okay. It's okay. Hang in there Tony, we're here for you."

Andrew and I had travelled by Qantas to be at Tony's bedside. On the flight, at first I was stony-faced, not wishing to break down in public. I failed miserably and sobbed from time to time. Andrew held my hand. A faceless airline flight attendant performed her job unobtrusively, fetching me glasses of water and tissues. I wondered what she thought. A family bereavement, probably. Well she was right. I had been slammed up against the realisation that my son was gone, never to return. The inner knowledge that this would be so, was intuitive.

As I looked at my son in his hospital bed, I thought his appearance was much the same as the last time I had seen him, which was more than a year earlier. As I put his hand between mine, I began to become aware of subtle changes. Tony's soft skin was now hairless and smoothly white. His nails were longer than I had ever seen them. They were manicured and shaped into a gentle curve. The moons were large and his cuticles pushed back. I was becoming aware of other subtle physical differences. Tony's hair was much longer. It was soft and as black as ever. Then I noticed there was no other bodily hair. Not anywhere, when previously Tony was quite a hairy man.

Tony was in a private ward with its own bathroom. Thank God, I thought. When we arrived I had expected to be offered some explanations, a few words of comfort, a touch on the arm by a nurse or a doctor. Something, anything, except what we actually encountered. The staff was friendly but after we explained which patient we were there to visit, they simply pointed us to the right room. They did not look us in the eye, or offer any assistance. I began to understand that the nurses on the desk could not handle the situation at all. They could not cope. However, we later discovered that the nurses actually assigned to attend to Tony were hand chosen and they looked after him with great tenderness and non-judgemental care.

I saw Andrew hold Tony close. They both sobbed quietly and I saw again the depth of distress in my eldest and my youngest sons' faces. Tony began to tell us about his life-long struggle to conform to his male body and to present a strong male persona to the world. He had, in recent years, taken up football again, in an attempt to force himself back into a macho role. Certainly he'd fooled his family. And me, his mother – I never, ever suspected, not for one fleeting moment, that my eldest son was anything other than a typically strong male member of our family, even though I always knew Tony had a very sensitive nature.

Apparently Tony had tried harder and harder to hide his own inner perception of being truly a female in the wrong body. He told us that occasionally he had cross-dressed and that his wife knew and thought it was all a bit of fun at first – dress-ups. Later she became concerned and told Tony he must promise never to do it again. Tony promised. He could not keep his promises.

We left the room for a while, promising to return as soon as we'd had a cup of tea in the hospital cafeteria downstairs. We walked along the corridor of a hospital built when money was more available for health care and when land was plentiful and cheap. The corridor seemed endless. We came to an area with small shops. This hospital serviced a huge area of Australia's largest state. Some people travelled hundreds of kilometres for treatment. Accordingly, facilities extended to cater for these needs.

We came to a bank, then a Medicare office. Out the front was a life-size cardboard cutout of a man dressed in drag. I believe the advertising slogan had something to do with 'changing' your medical insurance. The Hollywood type cardboard character looked like a cross between Mrs. Doubtfire and an escapee from Les Girls. Andrew and I could not control our mirth. The tension was released and we laughed all the way past the bank. How very appropriate, we thought, how absolutely, incredibly appropriate. From that moment we both knew we would need humour to help us to survive, though our laughter was short-lived at that particular time.

Tony's wife Judith arrived, coinciding with our return from lunch. Andrew and I returned to Tony and let him know we would be nearby, in a lounge room set aside for the use of visiting patients and their families, as a psychiatrist was due to speak to Tony and Judith and for a further consultation with Tony. The extreme act of castration that Tony

26

had performed on his own body was worrying, both for his family and for the medical staff. They were very concerned that Tony was in danger of further acts of violence to his body or even suicide.

I knew that Tony had already had a consultation with a Perth psychiatrist in the weeks prior to his hospitalisation. In fact, he'd rung me and told me of his dilemma. He told me the doctor had confirmed his own thoughts and made a diagnosis that Tony was indeed transsexual. I didn't understand at all and at that time was in total denial. I realised his marriage was floundering and would probably soon come to an end. I had even expected Tony to return to Melbourne. Then he'd have treatment and be better, I thought. At that time I had no comprehension of transsexualism. Even when we received the call that Tony was in surgery, my only concern was his recovery. And I thought that's how I would always feel.

Today, I have educated myself on the subject of transsexualism and know that my expectations of him at that time were totally unrealistic. I discovered that in the long-term, usually, a transsexual cannot deny their condition.

What causes transsexualism? Not even many of the so-called experts can agree. Theories abound. Toni has some theories of her own. One theory is expounded in a book called *Brain Sex*, which explains that part of everyone's brain matches itself to its own bodily parts. Transsexuals' brains do not match up with their own body. They feel they belong to the sex opposite from their body. This is a simplistic explanation of the theory and not a new one, except that in the book the author makes some suggestions about cause. One such explanation offered relates to the use of certain medications during pregnancy. The mother may have been prescribed something, particularly anything with hormone related drugs. Of course this theory does not hold water when probably there are transsexuals whose mothers never took any type of drug at all during their pregnancy. Other

27

theories I have heard relate to hormones the general population are ingesting through the food chain, such as what are fed to chickens to induce rapid growth. None of these theories explain to me why my son is a transsexual and it is something that I feel I must learn to accept, without concerning myself too much about its cause.

5

The First Week

Streetwise, Andrew urged me to walk close to him and on his right. He steered us to the centre of the pavement. "Keep away from the doorways and not too close to the gutter, Mum."

Apart from the years we had lived as a family in the suburbs of this city, Andrew had also spent two or three times living alone in Perth. He had learnt to take care of himself. Walking close to him now on a dark wintry night in the more seedy part of town, I felt safe. Though I confess it had not occurred to me to feel otherwise until Andrew pointed out the risks. At that moment I was especially glad my son was so tall. My naivety was ending. My education in many worldly things I wished I didn't need to know was beginning.

On the second night, after visiting hours at the hospital we decided, to save money, we would take public transport back to our apartment. In the morning we had succeeded in finding our way via two buses, so we figured it might be as easy to get home the same way. Wrong! The first bus trip from the hospital to the city was fine. But we discovered the next bus from the city along the river was finished for the night. We guessed there might be another way home via the central bus and train station.

While we walked, we talked. Neither of us had any previous knowledge or experience of what we were now facing. Although Andrew was more worldly and streetwise than I was he was only really accustomed to the straight, heterosexual side of life. Although there is a person in our family who is gay and we had come to accept that without a problem, Tony's difficulty was something else. The way I see it homosexuality is a sexual preference or predilection. Transsexualism is a misnomer because it is about gender; nothing to do with sex or sexual preference. It is a serious medical condition. The social worker had told me that if the condition is untreated, it may lead to various problems such as severe depression, drug or alcohol abuse, acts of mutilation (as in Tony's case) or even suicide. I had already read that the rates of suicide among the transsexual population are extremely high. I was worried about Tony's state of mind considering the drastic action he had taken and the self-mutilation he had carried out. Tony tried to explain to me that he did not consider it was mutilation at all. He was trying to make his body conform to what he felt that it should be.

Anyway, that day we had gone shopping for Tony to buy a few necessities. How proud I was of my tall son, Andrew, when we were looking for a dressing gown. "Mum, don't buy one in a man's colour, will you," he advised. His immediate sensitivity to Tony's needs far exceeded my own. I probably would have bought a dark blue gown regardless. So the hunt began. Tony is also tall, just on six feet. We knew we couldn't very well buy a totally feminine looking garment because Judith and other members of her family may be visiting. It was too soon for that. I can't begin to tell you how difficult it was to purchase just the right thing. Eventually we settled on a large white towelling, soft and fluffy dressing gown from the women's wear department of a large department store.

Razor blades were the next item on our shopping list. That was a real worry. We already understood Tony wanted to shave more than his whiskers. But was it safe to give Tony blades? A phone call to the staff at the hospital was embarrassing for us, but we had to ask. They suggested we buy packets of disposable blades and have the staff take care of them.

Of course the first thing Tony requested on our return was the razor blades. He wanted to shave. I explained that we had had to give them to the nurse. I asked her if we could have one. She insisted that I personally supervise Tony's shower and shave, another example of some of the staff having difficulty coping. There was no way I could intrude on Tony's privacy to that extent. And no way could I face seeing any wounds – although they were bandaged.

Tony whistled loudly while he showered and jokingly told me he wasn't going to cut his throat. I decided to reply in similar vein and said that it wasn't his throat I was concerned about. Andrew and I fell about laughing and Tony had a bit of a giggle as well. Recovery was beginning for us all, though the start was small. Never have I been so glad to see anyone come out of a bathroom as I was that day. It takes a long time for a hairy person to shave all of their body and Tony was in there for a long time.

On the morning of the fifth day following Tony's surgery we arrived to find Tony looking more concerned than he had been on the previous evening's visit.

"They're moving me today. To the 'psyche' ward." Tony informed us.

It seemed Tony's immediate physical needs had been cared for in the surgical ward long enough. They needed the beds and had decided to transfer Tony to the psychiatric ward of the same hospital – for observation. They could continue to care for his wounds there at the same time.

My return to Melbourne was imminent in the next couple of days. By this time I was becoming as much concerned for Andrew as I was for Tony. His detox was over, but he was still in the early stages of recovery and besides he was restricted by his court order that stated he must continue to receive treatment. I approached the hospital for assistance. They agreed to send a social worker to see us. Andrew had already committed himself to stay with Tony in Perth for as long as was needed. "You have to go home to Nana, Mum,"

Andrew said. And yes, I did. My mother's condition was still very serious indeed and I suspected that a lot was being kept from me. There was little more I could do for Tony in Perth at this stage and I agreed with Andrew.

A middle-aged woman social worker met us in a private part of the hospital garden. She was extremely kind and explained a little to us of the dilemma faced by transsexual people. How good it was to hear a person who at last was giving us encouragement and understanding. As far as Andrew's treatment was concerned, she couldn't really offer very much, as the hospital had no particular drug treatment programs. She suggested he visit a local G.P. who could supervise his medication. Andrew needed tablets for sleeping due to the long-term effects on his body from his habits. His nervous system needed time to recover. The G.P. could write a letter to satisfy the court in Melbourne that he was doing his best to comply.

The other concern I had in leaving Andrew behind was accommodation. We didn't know how long Tony would be in hospital and from the motel we were staying in it was awkward to get to the hospital by public transport. Besides I knew Andrew was very vulnerable at this stage of his rehabilitation and being alone in a large city at this particular time was not a good combination especially considering the stress he was under, facing his brother's problems. The social worker agreed to find a room in the hospital accommodation for country and interstate family members. That relieved my mind immensely.

When we returned to the surgical ward Tony's few belongings had been packed up and he was ready for transfer to the psychiatric ward. This was to be the next part of our long and arduous journey along the path to acceptance.

6

The 'Psyche' Ward

"Slow down Andrew. I can't keep up." Although Andrew
was pushing Tony in a wheelchair he didn't slow his pace.
He has such long legs and when he's nervous, he walks
faster than ever. I was lagging behind. We had already
walked a long way from the hospital accommodation which
was located fairly close to the surgical ward where Tony
had been and we were now striding the long corridor; at
least a kilometre from one end to the other. The rest of the
way we walked in silence apart from the sound of our shoes
squeaking on the polished floor and the slick noise of the
wheelchair's rubber tyres on linoleum. We kept our tentative thoughts to ourselves, each of us unsure about what the
new ward would be like.

The psychiatric ward was situated at the opposite end of
the hospital.

Glass doors with the ward number on them indicated our
arrival. We soon discovered that there were a few security
measures. Double doors were not locked during the day-
time, but were secured after visiting hours in the evening.

A round-faced male nurse wearing a large gold earring
in his right ear indicated that a more relaxed atmosphere
was the norm in Tony's new abode. He took us through the
formalities quickly, then steered us past the central nursing
station, the patients' sitting room and around a corridor to

Tony's ward. No private quarters here, five other patients shared the room. Tony was given the bed closest to the window – a blessing that at least afforded some measure of privacy in the large public ward.

I glanced around trying to 'suss' out the other occupants. All except one bed was empty. There were patients assigned to them, but it was mid-afternoon and they were elsewhere. One bed had curtains drawn around, though I could spy a teenage boy through the partly opened gap. A woman whom I guessed was his mother was trying to comfort the lad. He seemed exceedingly depressed.

Tony was to be assessed later in the afternoon by the resident psychiatrist, but for now he was free to sit in the garden or rest on his bed. As was Tony's restless nature, he couldn't wait to move around and see what his surroundings were like. We followed him to an atrium garden on the other side of the sitting room. Through a glass wall the staff could observe patients at all times whether they were inside or in the garden. It was much like being a fish in a bowl and I felt uneasy. Nevertheless we soon forgot our constant onlookers and chatted while observing the other patients as well as enjoying the outdoor experience after being cooped up with Tony in a closed surgical ward for days on end.

When the time came for Tony's consultation with the doctor, Andrew and I left, promising to return later in the evening. We had begun to make ourselves at home in the hospital and returned to Andrew's quarters before using the upstairs staff cafeteria for an evening meal. The warm smells of low-salt gravy, potato mash and over-cooked cabbage were nevertheless inviting following our steady diet for the last few days of sandwiches and pies. The food was very cheap as Andrew had been given permission to use the facility at staff prices while he was a resident on hospital property, for which we were very grateful.

When we returned after dinner we discovered that apparently the visit with the psychiatrist had proceeded well. Tony was cheeky enough to ask if it was permitted to smile while he was in the ward. He hadn't failed to notice the severely depressed state of several other patients. Though Tony was traumatised and already in grief over his broken marriage and the possibility that he may never see his children again, he was in remarkably good spirits.

"You've resolved something," the psychiatrist said. "As far as I'm concerned you don't even need to be in this ward. But we must keep you for a while to be sure you won't hurt yourself again. You're definitely transsexual and though you are depressed, you have begun your journey now and must work your way through many difficult times to come. You tell me you are going to Melbourne following your release. I will give you a referral to seek further treatment when you arrive there."

During that initial interview with the psychiatrist, he inquired as to how his parents and siblings were coping. Tony told the doctor of the many, many phone calls from his extended Melbourne family and of their long conversations and of their support. Then he stunned the doctor by telling him a private joke he had shared on the telephone with his father, which was really rather naughty. "I've lost a lot of weight, Dad" Tony said. Richard, quick as a wink, used rather black humour to bandy back, "Yes, two stones," referring to the loss of Tony's testicles. The psychiatrist almost fell from his chair he laughed so heartily. From that first consultation Tony and the 'shrink' were good mates.

However the next day something happened that frightened us all and even more so the staff in the ward. Tony was showering and part of his wound burst. He pressed the emergency button to summon help. As there was quite a lot of blood the poor nurse almost fainted with fright. She thought Tony had done himself a further terrible injury. Once Tony recovered his equilibrium from his own fright, I think he found some amusement in her discomfort.

7

She Ain't Heavy

Following my return to Melbourne, Richard travelled to Perth to be with Tony and Andrew for a few days. We exchanged brief telephone calls each day, so most of this part of my story is second-hand. I will tell you about it as much as I can in much the same way as it was related to me.

On a fold-down bed in the tiny room assigned to Andrew by the hospital, Richard slept close to his son. They were glad to be together and it provided time for Andrew to share the male perspective with his father. I know it must have been a great bonding experience for both of them, though neither has ever told me much about that side of things. But I saw a difference in their relationship from then on. Previously there had been a lot of angst between them, which somehow, from that time onward was gone.

Then it was time for Richard to return to Melbourne. Andrew was left to help Tony in the best way he could. And in every way he did. Tony had realised early on during his hospitalisation and probably long before, that his marriage was over. Judith wouldn't have him back, for even one day. That wasn't the way Tony wanted it to be. He had begged Judith to accept him as he was and continue their life together with the children. This was probably an unrealistic expectation to place on his wife. Though there are couples who have managed to stay together under similar circumstances it would take a very unusual woman for such a relationship to work, and this wasn't to be for my son and daughter-in-law.

Where would Andrew and Tony go? They could not stay in the hospital quarters once Tony was discharged. That was the rule. A social worker had come to visit Tony and helped him through the maze of applications for a sickness benefit. Unfortunately because Tony ran his own small printing business this was not easy, but a short-term assistance was eventually organised through Social Security. Andrew had only his unemployment benefit to manage on as well.

A small cabin in a caravan park not too far from Tony's home was finally secured for the time it would take to pack Tony's personal possessions and to pack up his business, which he worked from his home. This was going to be awkward as Judith, understandably enough, refused to be there when this was done. Nevertheless they managed to be civil enough to one another to arrange times for her to be out of the house so they could do whatever needed to be done. Tony was leaving his home, his wife and his children. How painful it must have been to return to his home and have to pack everything, when neither his mind nor his body had recovered from major surgery and massive blood loss, not to mention the trauma of his transsexual condition.

He could not lift anything due to his wounds and much of what needed to be packed was very heavy. Figuratively speaking Andrew carried his brother tirelessly and worked steadfastly alongside him, doing all the heavy work for the following three weeks – the time it took them to complete the necessary tasks.

Whenever the going became too tough, Tony and Andrew took a break. They told me about visiting a nearby bird park, a place Tony had often visited with his family. There they fed the colourful lorikeets and parakeets that were tame enough to land on their outstretched arms for seed. Black swans cruised close to the reeds of the nearby lake waiting for pieces of bread to be thrown to them. A simple barbecue meal of sausages and bread was shared with the swans.

For the most part, the organising of the move was planned in the cabin of an evening. They scanned newspapers for removalists and eventually settled on the cheapest and quickest quote that they could find. Within two weeks they had packed and sorted all of the business equipment and the few personal possessions Tony was bringing to Melbourne.

All of Tony's assets were signed over to his wife. This included the family home, two cars and all of the household furniture and chattels. In return Judith had agreed to allow Tony a final visit with the children. As Tony felt that he owed everything to his family, he was willing to forgo any rights to any assets, except for his business equipment. Unfortunately there was a sizeable debt attached to the business which he agreed to continue to pay until such time as their home was sold. This never was to be, but Judith did pay out what was left on the business loan when an arrangement was made to do with their property. I am not privy to that particular agreement. I am not sure that even Tony knows how her finances were managed. I do know that it was Tony's choice to give everything to his family. He felt they had, and would, suffer enough and it was the least he could do in the circumstances.

A meeting was organised between Tony and Judith for a quiet family meal at a local fast food outlet, where Tony could see the children for the last time before leaving for Melbourne. He has not seen the children since that day.

That night in the cabin, as you can well imagine, was as sad as a night can be.

Andrew could not comfort Tony and when he finally fell into an exhausted sleep, Tony dreamt the worst nightmares of his life. Andrew confided to me about the way Tony kicked the metal sides of the cabin walls at the side of his bed, tossing and turning, then calling out in his sleep. Once he actually screamed so loudly that Andrew was terrified. When Tony woke he told Andrew about a pig-man he'd been dreaming of, someone he feared very much and someone with the power to keep his children away from him forever.

8

Home Alone

Following my return to Melbourne, for a few days I had time for some respite. First stop though, was Epworth Private Hospital to see Mum. Miraculously the crisis had passed; it looked as though she was going to recover.

"Don't ask me how," her doctor told me. "It wasn't my skill that pulled her through. It was her will to live. She was this close, holding his thumb and forefinger almost touching, and I was sure we were going to lose her." He said this in front of my mother. I looked into her eyes and I understood she had fought to stay because she knew how very much I still needed her support at this particularly difficult time in my life.

Before going to Perth to be with Tony, I had to decide if, or what, to tell her. Knowing how ill she was made the decision all the more thought-provoking. What should I tell her? Knowing my mother, I came to realise that I must tell her the whole truth. She was well aware of how sick she was and she knew I would not leave her to go flitting off to Perth unless there was some extremely serious reason to do so. Then I briefly thought about telling a white lie, maybe that Tony was sick, but not exactly what was wrong. A social worker we had called in listened to us carefully. She said that perhaps we could tell her something, not everything. But she was wise. She insisted that I knew my mother better than they did and I should tell her what I thought was the right thing, no matter what her condition. That was great advice really, because it cemented my final decision. I already knew Tony would almost certainly be returning to live with us, at least temporarily. My mother would not appreciate finding out the full story later when perhaps it would be even more traumatic. So I told her everything before I left. I am convinced that's why she lived.

Although I was visiting Mum twice a day, there was still time left for me to be alone. This was what I needed. Time to weep. Time to think and to rest. Also I needed to prepare for the next few weeks at least. Arranging suitable sleeping space for everyone was high on my list of priorities.

Our home was comfortable, but fairly modest. We had only three bedrooms. Mum had one, Richard and I of course had our own room, which left one between Tony and Andrew. Before Andrew went to Perth he had been sleeping mostly in the lounge-room on the couch, as he was de-toxing. The other reason was that we had had a visit from Tony's daughter. She had only returned to Perth a couple of days before everything happened. The problem of finding enough bedrooms for everyone was eventually solved. We turned a small dining area into a space for Andrew. He willingly slept on a mattress on the floor in that tiny spot for five months so that Tony might have the other bedroom. Tony needed privacy as he was still healing physically, emotionally and mentally.

Several nights in a row during my time home alone found me soaking in a warm bath seeking solace. There I could let out my deepest feelings and sometimes I howled like a wounded animal. Other evenings, feeling calmer, I simply thought a lot about what might be ahead of us. It was all so confusing. That's when I began to question what I had done to cause Tony's condition. I suffered guilt, I felt sorry for myself. I worried about what other people would say, about what they would think and I thought so very many disjointed things. God got a fair bit of blame to wear. Why? Why? Why?

During that time I began thinking that a process seemed to have begun seven or eight years earlier where I was plucked up, set down and directed along a certain road. Call it fate, coincidence or some vast eternal plan, but some changes had begun that seemed to clearly lead me to a place that I needed to be. I was learning skills that would become essential for a particularly amazing journey in my life. As I lay in my bed alone at night I thought about all these things.

To explain, let me turn back the clock a few years. I had been working in the liquor store of a large and busy super-market. The work was heavy and my body objected. Shoulder and neck injuries forced me to leave. One day I told the manager to stick the job, though in actual fact I admit I used more polite words. 'My health is worth more to me than any job,' is what I recall I actually did say to him.

I was to have been placed on light duties, according to my doctor, but in fact that never happened. When I almost passed out with pain, I walked out in the middle of a shift. That was the first step that forged a new direction in my life.

A few days later my mother-in-law rang to tell me of a job in a small dress shop that she thought might not only inter-est me, but also provide me with lighter work. The next week I was selling dresses to old ladies in a 'frock shop' that was not only small, but also a very quiet, slow little business. During the winter especially I had many hours of solitude.

So I began to listen to talk-back radio or flicked to the A.B.C. to hear news of what was happening in the world. I began to take note of my lack of education and I was keen to learn whatever I could. I read more and more.

Every day on my way to work I picked up magazines and I began to complete crossword puzzles to help fill the lonely hours. Unknowingly my vocabulary was improving. I began to seek a creative outlet for one thing, but I soon realised there had to be more to a job than sitting behind a counter alone for hours on end.

I discovered while completing dozens and dozens of puzzles, that I had developed a love of words; their nuances and meanings became so interesting to me. I wanted to be able to use them. I wanted to write. But just then that idea had not clearly formed. It was just a vague sort of longing. What could I write? My life at that stage had seemed so boring. Right then while thinking of the past, I knew that eventually I would write about the events that were now shaping my life.

There were a couple more things that happened to me before I began to take up writing as a hobby. Although I couldn't imagine what sort of direction I should take, things just sort of happened. Fate pointed me toward this one path forward that I can clearly define only in hindsight. At the time I had no idea where I was heading.

Eventually boredom forced changes. I wanted to use whatever skills I had and I wanted to do something more useful in society than selling dresses. I read everything I could get my hands on in my spare time at work as well as doing puzzles and listening to radio.

One day I read an ad in the local paper for volunteers at a local agency. Soon I was completing a twelve-week training course and I found myself an interviewer at an information and referral bureau. During the completion of the training I was required to write an assignment. That was when I felt the first really defined need to write.

When I began work at the agency, one or two days a week, I had time to spare and I found a writing group at a local neighbourhood house. My tutor there fired my enthusiasm and inspired me to keep going.

One or two other skills were being learnt while I was hurtling faster than I realised to a time when all I was learning would become essential for my survival. It was around that time that we were finding Andrew's habits causing stress at home. Tension became unbearable and we heard of a twelve-step support program for families and loved ones of those with a dependency on drugs and alcohol.

Step one of the program says we are '… powerless over drugs and other people's lives.' Not only did this apply to myself in regard to Andrew, I soon discovered it meant so much more for me. I could use this principle to help me with Tony's dilemma and others in the family. As well, 'The Serenity Prayer' kept me going through tough times. The first line – 'God grant me the serenity, to accept the things I cannot change …' was so important to me. I began to stop being so involved in other people's lives and things that really did not concern me and I understood that I must accept whatever came my way. These were powerful lessons that I now knew would help me in dealing with Toni. I was becoming ready for the future, but I'm so glad I never knew what lay ahead of me.

While home alone I also found time to view the old black and white 'Mrs. Miniver' movie on television. I enjoyed every moment and savoured the quiet of the house. But it took a long, long time for me to recover from my grief and shock. Just then I wasn't yet ready for any acceptance. That would come much later. Counselling was what I needed now and immediately I sought whatever and whomever I could find to help.

The social worker I had met at Epworth had helped us greatly and she spoke to us at length on that first dramatic day. Amazingly we soon discovered she had had experience with transsexuals, so she was able to offer an understanding ear while comforting our initial distress. Her down to earth attitude was what we had needed at that time.

I had no idea where to begin to look for someone with knowledge that could help with counselling and/or support. Naturally I thought of approaching the social worker who already knew our story. My hope was that she might know of a support group for parents and family of transsexuals. She took time to look into this for me and discovered there was a group, but it was based in Sydney, which was no good to us. She also gave us the details of three support groups for transsexuals (or transgender people as some prefer to be known as). One group was called TLC, which stood for Transgender, Liberation and Care. For a long time I thought the initials meant tender loving care and that's exactly what it does stand for, though not really what the initials mean. 'Seahorse' is another group. The seahorse is an ocean creature with the ability to perform some of the roles of both sexes when procreating. The male of the species takes care of the eggs inside its body and gives birth to them. An appropriate symbol for the club, I thought. Some of the people who attend this club are also transvestites and crossdressers. There is also another club, which I fail to recall and I know little about. None of these groups specifically cater for the families of the affected person, though T.L.C. occasionally hold functions to which family or loved ones and friends are invited.

On the way home from seeing both Mum and the social worker at Epworth I visited the hospital chapel. Andrew, who I really didn't think had a single religious thought in his mind, had steered us into the chapel on 24th July, the day after we first received news about Tony's injuries. We had all stood quietly lost in our own thoughts and found comfort in the quiet room with the beautiful stained glass window.

So from that day whenever I was at the hospital I stopped in at the chapel. The window had a picture of an invalid man, held aloft by healing hands. I felt the man looked so similar to Tony that it was uncanny. He had a thin body, long arms and legs and silky black hair. I prayed while looking at that man. I am not a religious person, though I have a belief in God or a higher power, whatever one might choose to name that force. I think of myself as having more spiritual beliefs, than religious. On those visits though, I prayed for

Tony. I prayed for my family and I prayed for the strength to cope. I needed to be able to look after my mother when she came home from hospital while at the same time Tony would be returning, still unwell. I prayed for Andrew's continuing recovery from his dependency as well. For my husband, I prayed that he would be able to cope as well. He had been having problems for a while with his memory and other symptoms of a neurological nature. That was another concern that I had around that time. I'll tell you more about him later in my story. For now – I prayed for us all, including, and perhaps especially, for my grandchildren. My daughter-in-law was in my thoughts as well; I knew what a difficult time would be ahead of her, both as a single mother and in the unusual circumstances that had occurred.

9

Homecoming

The worst of Melbourne's cold winter was over. I was looking forward to spring and some of the sunshine I had tasted for a couple of days while I was in Perth. I was looking forward to Tony and Andrew's return, though with a somewhat tentative and nervous frame of mind. I knew there would still be some miserable, wet days ahead and I suspected that our lives would run parallel to the weather. I was right.

A 'midnight horror' or as it is sometimes referred to as the 'redeye' flight was due to land at Tullamarine airport a little after 5 a.m. Following a restless night, filled with mixed emotions we met Tony and Andrew at the airport.

It had not entered my mind to consider what Tony might be wearing when he arrived though I already knew he was not yet dressing full-time as a female. Nevertheless, I thought Tony looked rather oddly attired. He wore corduroy pants of a light orange-brown colour and his jumper was long, ribbed, and a brighter shade of orange. His longer hair and somehow more feminine appearance, with colours more reminiscent of the 'Orange People', made me swallow hard in surprise.

Tony's face was whiter than my own pale winter skin with a slightly jaundiced touch from the anaemia he had suffered from blood loss. On the other hand I had never seen Andrew look so fit and healthy, although he was weary and a bit bleary eyed from the trip. Also I noted how erect he stood, as though he had a new found inner strength and self-esteem.

As we settled in to living together, it was no more than a couple of days when, doing the family's washing, I discovered that underneath Tony's still fairly masculine clothing, he was wearing female underwear. That first time it felt strange, but soon I was sorting, folding and stacking his bras, panties and stockings without a second glance. That was what Tony wore now – simple as that. I surprised even myself at how quickly I adjusted to this small change in the family laundry.

For the first week at home, there was little for Tony to do, as he was waiting for his container load of goods to arrive from Perth. As soon as they came, Tony intended resuming the business. How that would be managed was another problem to be solved. A fair bit of space would be required to operate the small business from our home. We were already cramped.

An area of our family room was set aside as a small office; computer could go here, another desk there and shelving over that side of the room. We planned out the space before everything arrived. For the workroom that would be required we decided, following lots of discussion and some arguments, that our garage might suffice. It would mean parking our cars at the front and keeping the garage door permanently closed, but this seemed to be the only solution. Tony had no money to hire a small factory, which would have been the ideal situation. So it was that Tony, his business and his new life commenced in our home.

There was lots of time for talking that first week, and Tony loves to talk. Now that his secret life had become knowledge to all the family you could not shut him up. I did my best to listen patiently and I genuinely wanted to learn as much as I could about Tony's inner conflicts in an attempt to understand and make sense of what had been happening and what was happening now in my own head.

Transsexuals are quite an obsessive bunch, and I say that without malice and with great affection. It is simply the truth. They have a condition that is beyond my comprehension, so what must it be like to live their life? I cannot imagine. That was often what kept me going when Tony's chatter on the subject became a bit too much for me to bear. My initial reactions were that Tony needed every ounce of support that we could muster and that he was the one going through the worst dilemma I could imagine. It must have been a bit like being finally let out of a cage, when Tony revealed to the world what he had been living with for as long as he could remember.

Soon Tony would begin to dress more openly in female clothing. I knew that, but was wondering how on earth Richard would cope with seeing his son dressed in female clothing. Tony's brain told him that he really was female and he asked that we try to accept that as well. The other thing that Tony wanted was for us to begin to refer to him in the female gender. That, I can tell you, would take some doing and I will tell you more about that subject a little later as well.

Richard was in great distress and had very many concerns about Tony's future. He was worried that he could never be accepted as a female and that he might be regarded as a freak. He worried about his safety. He worried about how he could continue his business and whether clients would continue to offer work once they discovered the truth. He worried about his grandchildren. In fact his concerns were very similar to my own. But I think for a man, they are even more so. As far as using feminine terms to Tony, that was as yet impossible. But Richard found his love for his offspring far greater than any prejudice or preconceived notions he might have. He was eminently sensible, totally rational and a huge support both for myself and for the rest of the family. I loved him greatly for the way he conducted himself and how caring he was. That's not to say there weren't times of great conflict and plenty of times when he and Tony clashed.

During the week following Tony and Andrew's return, Mum was to be discharged from hospital. She was very weak and I knew she would need a bit extra care. Although I had looked after her before following previous episodes of quite severe illness, this time would be different. Not only did we have an over-crowded house and the stress of our family situation; Mum had now been placed on a home-oxygen life support system. That would take quite a bit of getting used to both for Mum and for myself. Anything new and mechanical has the ability to send me into a tail-spin, so I was scared about this equipment.

A rectangular-shaped brown oxygen concentrator was delivered to our door the day prior to Mum's discharge. She was to nickname this piece of equipment 'Alf'. She had nicknames for many things, but especially for all her invalid aids – her green walking frame she called 'Kermit'. The machine looked simple enough to operate and I was instructed in its use. Nevertheless I found the prospect of Mum using this contraption on a permanent basis, a daunting prospect.

At first the most annoying part of Mum's oxygen was the tubing. We were forever looking out for it, tripping over it and almost pulling the ears from her face. Never once did Mum complain, even when it must have hurt her when sometimes for the third or fourth time in a day we yanked on her tubing. She joked that she might be buried without ears by the time she was six foot under.

Mum's health at this time was very poor, but her spirits remained high. Wheezing and a constant debilitating cough were still causing us great concern. In fact it was less than two weeks before I once again had to call an ambulance.

Recalling this time I cannot help but laugh out loud about the farcical nature of the arrival of that ambulance in the midst of the complexities and drama of those early weeks. It seems to me now as if God had decided; just to add another extra little dimension, the road out front of our home should be remade at this time. I wish I were a talented cartoonist so I could draw a picture of the scene.

One side of the road was a foot or two lower than the other. Several earth-moving trucks and one delivering tar were all in the vicinity of our front garden. Also a large steamroller was working, flattening out the tar which had just been dropped in a heap. There were two men manning those 'Stop' signs on poles to direct the traffic. The stench and the dust were oppressive. In the midst of this chaos two ambulances arrived, one being the MICA unit which is always sent in cases of serious respiratory difficulty. Work out front stopped and we became the spectacle instead of the road works. What a grand entrance Mum made into the ambulance and what a bumpy ride she endured for a short distance.

10

Professional Prejudices

The Melbourne population was experiencing a typical late winter outbreak of 'flu. Perhaps not unexpectedly considering Tony's general health and his move from a warmer climate, he succumbed to a nasty bout of the bug. His state of mind was also causing concern as he was quite depressed. He was suffering nightmares and his evenings were filled with grief. Night after night alone in his room, he wept inconsolably for his children.

So when he was sick with 'flu I believe he felt the weight of all of his problems even more heavily. In fact he appeared to be becoming suicidal and unable to cope.

On the evening when he was most ill, Richard and I had gone to baby-sit our grandchildren, Paul and our daughter in law's children, when we received a distressing phone call. By then Mum was home again, so she rang telling us that Tony had collapsed and Andrew had to pick him up and carry him to bed. As soon as we could, we hurried home. I left Richard to care for Mum and I drove Tony to the emergency department of the local hospital.

Frantic about Tony's suicidal state and his 'flu, I blabbed to the black triage nurse expecting her to be both caring and understanding. For some reason I used to think people from minority groups and also those in the medical profession were blessed with superior human qualities of being accepting and non-judgmental of others. They of course are no different to any other people – some are kind, some are not. Anyway this nurse couldn't follow what I was trying to explain about Tony's castration, etc. Why I ever felt the need to tell her any of this at all I'm not sure. I think it was to do with my own confusion at the time and because I wanted her to know about Tony's anaemia and how urgent I thought it was for him to be seen by a doctor as soon as possible. The waiting room was full and I felt Tony would be unable to wait for a long time as he was extremely agitated. I was aghast at her reaction on hearing about what Tony had done to his testicles.

"What, both of them?" was what she replied in astonishment.

The whites of her eyes seemed as if they would pop out at any moment. She actually looked quite funny and I had to hide a smirk.

Following an even longer than expected delay we finally were ushered into a casualty cubicle. Again I wanted to explain to the Indian doctor the circumstances leading up to Tony's illness and the fact that I was worried about anaemia and also about him being suicidal. Can you believe his question, which I myself was stunned to hear him ask, "What, both of them?" His next question to me was whether I had brought Tony here to be treated for his 'flu or for his state of mind. (As if a doctor can't treat two things, I thought.) That night we left the hospital with neither a prescription nor a good opinion of the medical profession.

Looking back I find the episode hysterical. And amazing that two professional people should have such a similar reaction. Considering both the doctor and the nurse were coloured people it made me realise my notions of them being especially understanding were unrealistic ideas. And it confirmed my opinion that I now understood it makes no difference what race, creed or professional status people are, regarding their ability to be compassionate.

Another incident of bigotry by a professional person

happened when I presented myself at my usual medical centre for a consultation. I was having trouble sleeping (surprise, surprise!) and asked the doctor for medication. She asked why I needed it so I told her a few of the family problems we were experiencing. Her replies shocked and stunned me, particularly as it must have been fairly obvious that I was in a vulnerable state of mind. This doctor obviously had little, if any knowledge of the transsexual condition when I had thought that all doctors were familiar with this phenomena. Certainly she possessed no tact or compassion for me, her patient.

"Got a dysfunctional family, haven't you?" she bluntly told me. 'Well, tell me something I don't know,' I thought. What I didn't need just then was for her to state the obvious.

As far as Tony was concerned her comments were even more distressing to me. "Mad. He's insane. Must have been psychotic." Perhaps at the time he was but how insensitive can a doctor be? I walked out of her surgery with a prescription for sleeping pills in my hand and a resolve in my heart never to set foot in that doctor's room again.

What I did gain from that visit was the motivation to seek further counselling. I already knew that sleeping pills were a very temporary measure and that I needed other help. To the doctor's credit, she had spoken to me, though very briefly about counselling. She made no offers or suggestions as to where I might seek this treatment.

11

Transition

As Tony recovered from the 'flu and his strength began to slowly return, he and Andrew began work in earnest. It was about this time that we were in for a most challenging period of adjustment. Tony was beginning to transform himself into Toni, though at that stage she had not yet officially changed her name – that came a little later and caused quite a few hiccups, which is a chapter in itself. But for now her appearance was enough to give us quite a shock – you see, we had no warning.

One chilly evening following a delicious meal, we all settled to watch television together, content to relax and enjoy some viewing. Tony disappeared into his bedroom and came out dressed as Toni. I'm not sure how Richard reacted but he must have got as much of a start as I did. It was so unexpected. We didn't think Tony would begin to 'dress' so soon. She wore a long black stretchy gored skirt and black sheer stockings while on her feet she wore a pair of elegantly plain black court shoes. On the top half she added a simple white aran-knit jumper. Her hair was combed neatly into a more feminine style. Toni's face had been expertly made-up with a smoothly applied foundation, not too heavily, while on her lips was a delicate, natural lipstick. For her eyes she had used a touch of shadow and a little mascara. Her cheeks were pale with only a hint of blusher.

"What do you think, Mum?" she asked, looking at me for approval.

I had to admit she didn't look half bad. Apart from her balding head, she might pass quite well as a woman. While I told Toni what she wanted to hear, and I did mean it, inside I was a quivery mess. I knew I would take a long time to accept my son, as I still thought of him then, dressed as a woman.

You will notice that I have begun to refer to Tony in the feminine gender. Well, I did try. That fluctuated from day to day and from one hour to the next, so as I tell you my story you will understand the swing from he to her, from Tony to Toni, depending on how I felt and how I was coping at that particular time. Also the computer in my head had been saying 'he' for almost thirty-five years. I could not change overnight any more than Tony could.

Male pattern baldness was an impediment to Toni's transition that was causing her great distress. She worried, fretted and moaned to me about her hair, until I could just about scream. Though I sympathised with her predicament I held no magic solution in my motherhood bag. "What about a wig?" was the only suggestion I could offer.

Andrew must have become as fed up as I was about hearing about hair and about whether a few more strands had fallen out. Or sick of hearing questions such as, 'Does it look better this way?' or 'Would it be more concealing if I comb a fringe across?' because the next Saturday he went shopping with Tony to Prahran.

I knew Tony had a magazine with pictures of female wigs in his possession that he'd brought with him from Perth. He'd sent for the mail order catalogue some time ago. Leafing through the booklet we attempted to be as helpful as we were able and made comments about whether a similar colour to his own hair would be best, should it be curly, long or short, with or without a fringe. It was such a strange situation for us at that time to be offering ideas about what sort of female wig Toni should wear.

Without a word about where they were going on that particular Saturday, off they went. Tony was dressed in his normal
day wear of jeans and a shirt, looking almost as masculine as
any other male you might see in a day's outing. You see, Toni
was not confident to appear in public because of the 'hair
problem'. So unbeknown to me, Tony and Andrew went shopping for a wig for Toni.

Imagine my surprise when they returned and Tony had
long red hair. He looked quite unusual, I can tell you, with
as much male appearance as ever, except for his head which
was adorned with the new wig. I dutifully admired the wig
and told him I liked the colour, which I did. It was a fairly
subdued auburn shade, perhaps not what you would really
describe as 'red' though I tend to refer to people with
auburn hair as red-heads. I felt the texture of the new wig
and clucked around a bit, trying to provide Tony with the
confidence he was seeking.

About an hour later Toni emerged from her bedroom.
This time the female persona was achieved quite well.
Styling of the wig would take a little time. Toni, I thought,
didn't have the front combed quite right, but I needed to be
very careful about comments as Toni was more than a little
touchy on the subject and unable to accept criticism very
well no matter how good the intention. I soon found the best
thing to do was to keep quiet and allow Toni to make her
own decisions about her appearance. It would take trial and
error and although Toni often asked my advice I was reluctant to say much to her at all in regard to her dress. If I saw
something that was very obvious, occasionally I ventured a
suggestion, but not very often.

A new wardrobe of clothing was Toni's next priority. She
had some underwear, as I've mentioned, but apart from
those few items, her clothes were all male. Toni's intention
was to begin to 'dress' full-time as soon as possible. But while
she was working during the day, her clothes were mostly
male, though gradually she discarded the most masculine

looking of those and chose colours that were more feminine from his already existing wardrobe. This was an androgenous sort of period as far as her appearance.

In the bedroom, which was previously a spare room, was a wardrobe which housed the over-flow of my own clothes, mostly things that were now too small for me, but being a bit of a magpie, I was reluctant to part with. For Toni it must have been like an Aladdin's cave. The first time we'd seen Tony as Toni, I'd noticed she was wearing one of the skirts from my wardrobe. I didn't particularly approve of this, once I realised she'd been trying on my old clothes, so we made a pact. I would give her what she wanted, if they fitted. If I gave her something, it would be hers. I didn't want to share any of my clothes. This was a hard step for me. Clothes are my passion and in the circumstances, it felt weird for Toni to wear anything of mine. I think Toni realised how I felt then and she respected my wishes. It was just that she was so desperate to transition and she had no female clothes to wear.

The next weekend Toni asked me to go shopping with her. She wanted to buy some high-heel shoes and a skirt. She had very little money at that time, but what she did have was ear-marked for whatever was required to transform her appearance from male to female. That included the wig, clothing and, before long, treatment for facial hair removal. At present Toni was using razor blades, but she wasn't satisfied with them on a permanent basis.

My heart dropped and my nervous stomach flinched. She wanted me to go out with her to a local shopping centre? As Toni? I did my best to hide how I felt and agreed. That was the most difficult shopping expedition I have ever experienced. And I love shopping.

Exactly how Toni was dressed that morning escapes me, but I do remember she wore a short skirt and sheer, black stockings with high heels that she already had. That pair of shoes was too high, she felt, and they hurt. She intended buying another, more comfortable pair to fit her size 10 ladies feet. As a man Tony wore only about a size 8.

The resolve in my head and my heart was strong not to allow anyone who might be unkind, who stared or sneaked a second look, or perhaps worse, might make, snide comments, to upset me. I thought Toni had as much right to go shopping for clothes as any other person. She is a human being with the same blood and the same emotions inside her as every other shopper in the centre. But as this was my first time, as well as Toni's, it wasn't an easy expedition for either of us, and my logical thoughts were soon taken over by my old-fashioned and sheltered background notions. My son looked different and I wasn't used to him being female.

Before Toni entered our lives, I probably would have snuck a second look myself if I'd been out and had seen someone like her, maybe I'd have given a little snigger or perhaps even felt a bit threatened. Now with my daughter, I expected people to react otherwise, even though I know it's only human nature to notice a person who looks a bit different.

Toni didn't want to be different. She wanted to be like any other woman out on a shopping spree. She wanted to blend into the crowd. But for now my daughter needed more time before she would 'pass' fully as a woman.

We had discussed where we should go shopping and we both decided that, although Toni might be accepted more readily in some of the trendier inner suburbs, this was where we lived and we might just as well accustom both ourselves and the regular shopkeepers to Toni. That way, once the first time was over, we figured it would become easier. That seemed to have been one of the wisest decisions we made.

First stop was PB Shoes shop. Forever I will remember fondly the salesgirl, though I wouldn't recognise her again if I fell over her. She was more than kind. She gave Toni not even a second glance, though at that time Tony's male body was fairly obvious. The girl had endless patience and hunted for the most suitable shoes for Toni's feet. Luckily, she doesn't take a huge shoe size, as some of the other 'girls' do, so that was no problem. Eventually Toni settled on a pair of plain black pumps with a lower, more solid heel, in which she could feel, and walk, more comfortably. We had a quick look around for a skirt and bought a few food essentials. By then, we'd both had enough.

That was the day of Princess Diana's funeral. We all sat together as a family with Toni and watched till the early hours of the following morning. Like much of the population we were drawn to the Diana saga, and personally I admired her very much. I felt the only consolation of Diana's death was that she would forever remain young and beautiful. Oddly enough, it had been fairly recently, when admiring her beauty on a magazine cover, that the thought entered my head that before we know it, our beauty fades. As I was past fifty years old myself, I had watched my own wrinkles begin to appear. My grey hair had long since been hidden by the dye from a bottle. "What a pity she'll get old too," I had thought.

We all had tears for Diana but I silently grieved the loss of my son. I cannot adequately express the confusion of grieving the loss of a son, while she was sitting next to me as my daughter. In a way it was therapeutic to be able to cry so openly in front of the family while lost with my own secret thoughts. Probably that sounds rather strange, but that's how it was for me on the night of Diana's death. Of course I had times of crying alone, or with Richard, but the comfort of the family around me and all of us feeling a bit sad together was helpful. Even though no one knew my innermost feelings, it was a great release. In a way it was a symbolic funeral. They didn't know what I was suffering and I had no wish for them to know.

That day out shopping, then watching Diana's funeral, marked one of many turning points in my journey to acceptance. We all became accustomed to Toni's more frequent visits. Most evenings now she was appearing as Toni, but then sometimes just as soon as she had arrived, she would have a bath and emerge in warm pyjamas, minus make-up and wig, ready to go to bed as Tony. Not only was this period a transition time for Toni; it was for her family as well.

12

Business As Usual

During a lull in the road construction work at the front of the house, Tony's container-load of possessions arrived. It was very quickly unloaded into our garage. But as Tony was still unable to lift anything heavy, Andrew did the bullock work. Tony worked just as hard at organising, setting everything up and unpacking the smaller items. They proceeded to transform our two-car size garage into a small factory workshop.

This was no easy achievement. It was still cold and wet. One side of our garage was only separated from the swimming pool by a wire fence. The roof leaked and there was insufficient light to see well enough for their printing business. Although Tony had run his small business from his home in Perth the conditions were more suitable there. He had a triple garage, fully bricked, with plenty of fluorescent lighting. Off to one side of his garage he'd had his office/computer room. Here in Melbourne that had to be inside the house as our garage was not only too small, it wasn't sufficiently weatherproof. Nevertheless, they found a way, and before long had rigged up lights, fixed the leaky corrugated iron roof and covered in the open side with makeshift tarpaulins.

Now they were ready to commence work. There was much to be done. Andrew had helped Tony on previous visits he'd made to Perth, so he had a limited knowledge of the work. Tony duly appointed Andrew as a partner and new director in the business. He would learn as they worked and although he was now a senior partner he would also be Tony's apprentice, learning on the job.

Mostly their system worked quite well. Tony would be inside in the area of the family room that we had converted into a small office, seated at the computer, either setting up the printing job to be done next or contacting clients, or doing the necessary bookwork. All of Tony's clients needed to be contacted, as he had been out of action for several weeks now. Some jobs were over-due and other clients had been neglected. It was important to keep approaching his clients so that the work kept coming in. Now there would be two wages to pay.

As Andrew had been unemployed for a long period of time, he was eligible to apply for a government subsidy to be paid to an employer. That was duly applied for and received. It paid most of Andrew's wage for about five months, which gave them breathing space to make the business again profitable.

"What should I tell them, Mum," Tony asked, in reference to his absence and the delays in finishing work for his customers. I suggested he tell them he had been in hospital for a big operation. That was true. And for the time being, that was all that Tony was prepared to say. He rang most of his customers or sent change of address cards to those he had not had work from for quite a while. The fact that the business had transferred 'over east' was another stumbling block. Tony needed to convince everyone that he could continue the same standard of work, get it to them on time and at the same cost.

For the most part, clients were prepared to give Tony a go. After all he had been doing work for them for several years now and they were fully satisfied. Later on a few clients pulled the plug, for a couple of reasons. One client, once they knew about Tony's change to Toni, simply refused to offer work to someone 'like that'.

Then there were one or two customers who wanted to give work to Western Australian companies. There is a fair bit of parochialism between Western Australia and the 'Eastern States'.

Andrew managed to learn the job quickly, but there were times when he became impatient, needing Tony's help immediately, when he was busy in his office. This presented a fair bit of stress all around. Our home was open-style and usually I was in the kitchen at the other end of the family room, while Mum would be snoozing in her armchair in the centre of the room. Sometimes she wanted to watch television while they were working and Tony was on the telephone discussing business. It wasn't easy for any of us, but for the present we had to make the best of it. The business must go on.

A long convalescent period for Mum meant lots of hospital and doctors' visits. This at least got us out of the house for a while and we enjoyed the break from being cooped up in the middle of the workshop, office cum family room.

Once a week my cousin came and sat with Mum, while I went to do the voluntary social type work that I enjoyed. My job entailed, among other things, offering a listening ear to other people's problems and giving pre-counselling to them or suggesting referrals that may be appropriate for their particular need. Some family members and some friends wondered how I could do this work when so much was going on at home and thought it must be too stressful for me. I disagreed. In fact I felt it was therapeutic to listen to other people's worries knowing there were worse things that could happen to a family, much worse, and I seemed to be more empathetic than I was before. Besides, I didn't consult with any of my clients on an on-going basis, which may have been too hard for me. My work entailed only 'one-off' interviews with people I would more than likely never see again. Only rarely would you see the same client again, and then it would be a long time between visits. So I continued my work and my life in much the same way as it was before.

As for Richard, he was an executive, and had worked for the same large company in the food producing line, for more than thirty years. Previously I alluded to him having difficulty with his memory. The stress of what was happening at home wasn't helpful, but we came to discover later that he was suffering a neurological illness, and although the stress had a bearing on his condition it was in no way the cause of his memory loss. But just then, we didn't know what was wrong. In fact, although I had noticed, his boss had noticed and Richard had worried about himself recently, no-one else thought there was anything at all the matter with him. He kept on going and went to work every day as usual and nothing altered too much at that particular time. It was business as usual for the whole family.

13

The Team

From the first day of Tony's arrival back in Melbourne, I knew his intent was to seek acceptance as a patient in the 'gender reassignment program' which he knew would entail an assessment period of approximately two years.

At the time Tony was very impatient. Not only to begin seeing the team, but to realise his dream of becoming Toni. Somehow Toni had found the contact number in Melbourne for the treatment she was seeking. I think some of the information that she already knew had been given to her by the psychiatrist in Perth. She asked me to ring and try and secure an appointment for her. Although I was reluctant to do this, I knew the reason she didn't want to do it herself. Her voice was still deep and masculine sounding and she was very conscious of not being accepted on the telephone.

Toni had been practising secretly for a long time; learning tricks and inflections of speech that would make her sound more feminine. "Do I sound okay?" she asked, for the umpteenth time. I was not impartial enough to really be able to judge whether her voice would pass reasonably well or not. Usually I agreed that she sounded fine. It was easier that way. Sometimes white lies were the best way for me to cope. As long as Toni lives, I don't think that to me she will sound much different, though more softly spoken now and with a somewhat higher pitch to her voice.

So for the sake of peace, I agreed to ring the clinic. The woman who answered had a very deep voice. I guessed that the receptionist was probably transsexual and I actually thought Toni sounded much more feminine than she did, but obviously she wasn't as concerned about her voice as Toni was. I managed to obtain the information required. To be given an appointment, Toni must first of all acquire a referral from a Melbourne doctor. She would need copies of her psychiatric reports from Perth and she would need to write a letter herself, stating why she wanted the appointment. Another requirement was a photo of how Toni looked at this time. The receptionist asked to speak to Toni and I called her to the telephone. That let me off the hook and from then on I vowed she would have to do this for herself. It wasn't my place to do any of it for her. After all I felt I was having enough difficulty coping.

My G.P. already knew what had happened to Tony in Perth, so I suggested that she might be a good starting point as Tony needed a referral to the gender re-assignment clinic. Amazingly, this doctor had been present at one of the very first sex-change operations in Melbourne. She told me all about that time in her training during my first visit to her when I was so distressed. Back in the 1970s the surgery was performed in a large Melbourne hospital, in the centre of the city. The operating theatre was locked to any unauthorised staff. No one, save a few of the staff who were directly involved, knew what was going on. It was all top secret. My doctor was very young then and was an observer in the theatre. She was advised of the total confidentiality of what was happening. No one was to know that this hospital was performing sex-change operations, as they were commonly referred to back then.

As Tony had been diagnosed as suffering 'gender dysphoria' or 'gender identity disorder' as it is more often referred to these days, the G.P. had no problem in providing the necessary referral to the gender dysphoria clinic.

Family support was also one of the things the doctors were seeking as another positive for candidates applying for surgery. Therefore I offered to write a letter to the team, to be added to the rest of the paperwork which they required. This is what I wrote –

Dear Doctor K...,

A few weeks ago my eldest son, Tony Langley, confided to me, then shortly afterwards to other members of our family and to his father, the problems he was suffering with his male gender.

As a mother I was stunned and in shock. Tony is my son, yet I was in total ignorance of his dilemma. All his life, since he was tiny, I was aware of 'some-thing' and always afraid for him, somehow knowing there was some hidden agenda within him. Only now do I know what has been the cause of his distress – his recently diagnosed 'gender dysphoria'.

Tony has been living in Perth for many years with his wife Judith and two children, Hannah, 9 years and James, 4 years. Distance has presented no bar to family ties. We are closely bonded to our grand-children. My daughter-in-law Judith, has always been kind, loving and polite to my husband and I, but we have, for a long time been aware of a deterioration in their marriage.

Last month Tony's marriage ended. Unable to cope with his 'gender dysphoria' any longer, Tony removed his testicles and almost bled to death.

Somehow I had clung to the hope that Tony would work through his condition by seeking treat-ment, leaving Judith and returning to Melbourne in an amicable parting. This was not to be. Tony has now returned to Melbourne following his recent hospitalisation in Perth and is now living with us temporarily while he organises his business, his

68

accommodation and begins the treatment that he wishes to have.

I am struggling with the changes Tony wishes to make. That does not mean there is any lack of support; to the contrary, I feel a certain relief in knowing what has been bothering him and I am his mother whether he is male or female and love him immensely. He is a wonderful person and deserves every drop of happiness he can squeeze from the rest of his life. The path won't be smooth, but this is Tony's journey and I believe he will find his way.

I can tell you about the overwhelming loving support and the number of messages and visits Tony has had from his family in Melbourne. His two brothers have both been loving and supportive. Paul is struggling a little but is totally there for Tony and is broad-minded in his attitudes. Andrew has been as close as a brother could be to Tony. Andrew has now become a business partner of Tony's as well.

We have a large extended family and many long telephone conversations between Tony and various family members have all been supportive. Aunts, uncles, cousins, grandparents, even an old girlfriend, have rung Tony offering comfort and love.

Richard, Tony's father, has been coping reasonably well, considering he admits himself to holding some narrow-minded, somewhat bigoted attitudes. He is working towards his own changes and acceptance of Tony. He loves Tony and has watched programs on television and discussed 'gender dysphoria' with me, in his efforts to understand what is happening. I know he will find Tony's change difficult, but I believe, as Richard does, that love conquers all.

As for myself, yes, I will, I do, I am finding the going a strain at present, but with love, education about the condition and confrontation with my own feelings, I feel I am coming to terms with the prospect of expecting the re-birth of Tony to Toni.

With kind regards,

Lynda Langley.

Little did I know how difficult the road ahead would be when I wrote this letter to the head of the 'gender dysphoria' clinic. I dare say if I had to write the letter now, the wording may be slightly different. Basically nothing has changed; it's just that I didn't realise how rough and bumpy I would find the path of life.

Weeks passed, with Toni growing more and more anxious about whether or not she would be granted an appointment with 'the team'. Eventually a letter arrived. Tony was on the one hand ecstatic that she had been given a first appointment with the head of the team, a psychiatrist. On the other, she was upset about the three-month wait until her turn to be seen. To her, it must have seemed an eternity. At least that's the way she behaved. Her insecurities were huge. Would they continue to treat her? Would they accept her? Would they eventually pass her as a suitable candidate for gender re-assignment? Toni's constant worrying wore me down. I did my best to be supportive, but I assure you it was not an easy task. The two-year wait for surgery was too long, according to Toni. She would just die, if they made her wait that length of time. And if they didn't pass her for surgery, she would definitely die, because she said she would kill herself. By then I felt like saying to her, 'Well hurry up and do it then, before I get to that state of mind as well.' That might sound uncaring, but really it was such a difficult time and she was so hard to listen to sometimes.

At long last the big day arrived – Toni's first appointment with Dr. K…

There was much worry about what she would wear, how she would style her hair and about make-up. I recommended, often, that less is more as far as make-up is concerned. But at that time Toni was extremely conscious about her facial hair and tried to cover up with thick foundation. Often this only accentuated the problem. However I could not convince Toni to use less. So, I gave up and let her do her own thing. My worry was that she might be even more conspicuous with heavy make-up.

I waited nervously for Toni's return. By now, I had become so involved with the whole process that I paced, worked furiously at the housework and tried every way I could to distract myself while she was gone. When she returned, I wished I had enjoyed the peace and quiet of the time she was out. Because she went on and on about the visit for the next couple of hours.

"She's a bitch," were Toni's first words. "Do you know what she said, Mum?"

"No, what?" I replied.

With that Toni mimicked the doctor's educated voice, and I confess she had me in hysterics. 'You'll never be a woman, you know. It's all an illusion.' The word illusion was long and drawn out and I laughed aloud.

Toni ranted a bit about being an 'illusion', but she was well aware of what kind of response was expected from her. She told the psychiatrist that she understood that and that the best she would ever hope for was to be accepted and to look and be as much female as she could possibly be; to make her body match who she had felt like inside for most of her life.

I can't say for sure what was in Toni's head, but I suspect she lied. I think perhaps that she thought that she *would* be a woman, in every way, once they performed the requested surgery. As I said, I'm not privy to Toni's thoughts, this was my own opinion. But I think by that time I had become quite fey about the transsexual mind. I knew very well that

Doctor K... must be in tune with all of their little tricks as well.

For some time Toni related to me all of the questions, and her responses to them. It sounded to me like she had handled herself quite well. For the most part I think she had been very honest with the doctor.

Doctor K..., of course, was concerned by the extreme act of castration which Tony had performed and why he had done it. Tony agreed that he had suffered a breakdown and must have been a bit insane at the time, but that his condition had caused him such distress and he had become so confused at the time that he could see no other way out. I've never actually discussed with him why he did it. This was what he told me that he discussed with the doctor. She said to Toni that this was the first case she'd come across in all the years of her practice where such a thing had happened. She knew of cases overseas, but of none in Australia. Not to her knowledge anyway. At least this was what she told Toni. Much later on, Toni claimed to have heard of at least one other person in Australia, who had attempted a similar act of castration.

The whole consultation, it seemed to me, was a testing process. Dr. K... had been a bit rough on Toni, baiting her, to see what her reactions were. This was my interpretation of what had happened, from what Toni related to me. I was, of course, only guessing, but I told Toni how I saw it in an attempt to console her.

"She's testing you Toni. She needs to know what your state of mind is now and whether you are suffering from any other mental illness, such as schizophrenia."

I thought that probably the doctor was worried that Toni might do something else to harm herself. I'm sure Toni didn't confide in the doctor about the episodes of feeling suicidal, though I already knew the high rates of suicide among transsexuals. As head of the team, no one would have been more informed about those statistics than Doctor K... I then asked

Toni if she had told the doctor about her suicidal feelings and she smiled and simply said, "Do you think I'm mad." She didn't want to say anything that might delay her cause – gender re-assignment surgery.

There were several members of the team. I already knew that Toni would be required to be assessed by two independent psychiatrists, be seen by an endocrinologist, have a general health check and many blood tests to exclude conditions such as HIV positive status and hepatitis, just to name a couple. As well, she was to undergo a series of psychological tests, to assess her suitability for surgery. After all, once surgery was completed, there would be no going back. In my own mind, I was convinced that Toni would be passed, once the necessary processes had been served, particularly as she had already performed an 'orchidectomy' on herself.

The second psychiatrist was an elderly man who had been working with the transsexual community for many, many years. In fact I later discovered in a newspaper article printed about his work that he had been 'father' to many of the modern ideas regarding these very special people. I believe he has a great regard for transsexuals. He was one of the first doctors to put forward the notion that they were not at all 'mad', that in fact there was something amiss within their brain that convinced these people that their body didn't match up with their true gender identity.

I remember that for the first few times Toni saw him, she had a fairly negative attitude to him as well. She thought he was 'too old' and 'past it' and 'an old fuddy-duddy'. Later she changed her mind and became fond of him. Toni's relationship with Doctor K... was also a happier one as they got to know one another.

It came as no surprise to either psychiatrist that Toni had not been able to wait to see the endocrinologist before commencing hormone treatment. They would have preferred that she had, but of course they were very experienced doctors and they knew that most of the transsexuals who came before them had already taken matters into their own hands in regard to commencing hormone treatment.

Toni had started her 'pretty pills' as she sometimes referred to them, a few weeks before her first appointment with Doctor K... I had been against this, but obviously, mothers know little. I attempted to mind my own business anyway and let her do whatever she wanted. After all she was almost thirty-five years old and considering the drastic action she had already taken, what further harm would a few hormone tablets cause?

Where she would obtain a hormone prescription, I had no idea. Toni did. She had been using the internet for all kinds of information and the transsexual community were not slow in providing information to one another via modern technology.

A 'quack' doctor, as I at first referred to him, had given Toni what she asked for. There were many changes happening in my mind as I progressed along the path of Toni's treatment and I began to understand that the doctor who first prescribed hormones to Toni wasn't really a quack at all. In fact he was a very compassionate person who understood the dilemma that these people face in their lives.

He took Toni's blood pressure and did appropriate blood tests at the time he gave her the prescription. So I believe he was taking all the care that was required. This was confirmed when Toni saw the endocrinologist at the hospital. The specialist performed a full work-up of Toni's physical condition, and agreed that the hormones Toni was already taking were quite suitable.

The hormone tablets, Toni hoped, would promote breast growth, soften her facial skin and round out her features. Perhaps she expected small miracles. It took a long time for anything to happen and again Toni's already impatient nature was sorely tried. She explored the internet for hormones that would quicken the process and she soon discovered a great deal of information on the subject. After quite a long period on one particular type of tablet, she tried some others, then another, then another.

Eventually she settled on tablets and a weekly injection of hormones. They worked and breast growth progressed. I've never seen her breasts, though Toni has offered to show me. They are not something I am yet able to see. Being a modest sort of mother, I didn't feel I needed to see for myself what was happening, though I have on occasion noticed Toni wearing a T-shirt without a bra and she definitely has got breasts. For a long time she wore 'falsies' or Kylie Minogue style push-up bras. Now she is content to wear an average type of bra for most day wear.

So for the next twenty-three months Toni continued on her program towards her ultimate goal – gender re-assignment surgery. There were very many hospital, clinic and doctor's visits. Often we walked the road alongside her. When the time came closer to her approval for surgery, I even went with her to the surgeon's office. She needed transport and I was curious to catch a glimpse of the man who performed this God-like surgery. Although I didn't actually go into the consultation with Toni, I did see the surgeon that day and I noticed him glance my way. Perhaps he was wondering what the mother of a transsexual looked like.

14

Out Raging

"What on earth are they doing in the bathroom?" Richard asked, irritation beginning to irk him.

I didn't know and wondered myself. Toni and Andrew had been in there a long time, together, and with the door closed. That was unusual. They never went into the bathroom together. And especially not with the door shut.

Our curiosity was answered when Toni threw open the door with stage-like abandon to display her totally bald head. My eyes were stunned. I didn't know what to say. Eventually I managed a feeble, "Why?"

It was simply a matter of comfort. The weather was becoming warm as summer approached and Toni couldn't stand the constant heat and the itching that her wig was causing. Andrew must have had to listen to her complaints while they worked outside under the hot tin roof of the garage. Being the practical one of the family, I think it must have been him who suggested to Toni that she shave her head. Well, I think she got a fair bit of help from Andrew in the actual process. I had heard quite a few giggles coming from behind that closed door.

I didn't know whether to laugh or cry and didn't dare do either for fear of upsetting our 'prima donna'. Toni was very touchy about her appearance. It was so important that she 'pass' as well as she could. I said I understood how hot it must be to wear a wig. Of course I didn't, never having worn one, but one can imagine.

Nightclubbing had come to be a part of Toni and Andrew's weekends by now. There was always a great deal of fuss over what to wear. Toni had been given a pair of black leather trousers and she'd bought a black crop top with a row of stretchy lace that fitted under the bustline. She looked a bit way out for my liking and far too sexy, but nevertheless I suppose she was fine for a nightclub. The long red wig had been styled to beyond an inch of its use-by. In fact it wasn't long before Toni bought another one. She had cut off bits of the original wig and it was beginning to look a bit like a rug the dogs had got hold of and chewed the fringe.

Within weeks of Toni's arrival in Melbourne, she had found her way to a support group. T.L.C. was the one she chose as being for 'true' transsexuals. Soon Toni had friends like herself. To my surprise some of the members liked to rage. Don't ask me why it was a surprise. I think I expected Toni to settle into a sedate life as a female, similar to the life Tony had already led. Perhaps I thought other people like her were the same. As it turned out, Toni had been set free to explore a whole new world. As Tony had married young and worked tirelessly building homes and a family in Perth, he'd never really had time to go out and rage. Now Toni was making up for lost time.

Andrew still liked to have a drink and didn't need a great deal of coaxing to go along with Toni. It was a great new and exciting scene that neither of them had ever experienced before. I discovered there were a couple of pubs that ran nights attended by transsexuals. At the nightclub there were a variety of patrons. These clubs were a meeting place for transsexuals but there were also drag queens, a few cross-dressers, gays, transvestites and anyone else who was out for a good time. The gawkers, I suspect, soon got shifted along.

My own knowledge of these clubs was all second-hand. Toni and Andrew loved to tell me all about their experiences.

They were having a ball. Toni was making new friends all the time and finding her feet in the big city. As well it was a fantastic time in their lives. They were stressed getting the business under way and working hard every day, so at the weekend they really enjoyed their time off.

At first I was petrified about Toni and Andrew going out late at night. I was concerned for Toni, thinking she may face discrimination. I was worried that Andrew would always protect her and even though Andrew would avoid confrontation, as he was a very peaceful person, I knew that, under the influence of alcohol and with sufficient provocation he could look after himself. I abhor violence and the very thought of any trouble was on my mind every time they went out clubbing.

The other worry, which concerned me out of all proportion, was the toilet issue. If they were going to a gay place that didn't worry me much for Toni. They were all broad-minded enough not to care who used the 'ladies' or who used the 'gents'. But then I was thinking about whether Andrew might have any trouble. He is straight and I didn't know how he might react if anyone should approach him. I figured he was big enough to look out for himself, though I suspected he was a bit out of place at some of these venues. I think he coped by having a few extra drinks.

Before long I realised that Andrew had been well accepted as Toni's brother and I think that the transsexual community all took care of one another. And Andrew was now 'one of them' as a family member. I had learnt not to concern myself about the toilet arrangements any longer. Although I knew there were no difficulties in certain places, in the general community there still could be a problem. But there never was.

The first time Toni and Andrew went out to the casino I spent the night worrying, again about toilets. Toni told me the women were marvellous. Although a couple had 'read' her – the term used by transsexuals which refers to the times

78

when people can pick that they were not born to the gender they are now dressing – they were kind enough not to say a word. I think women are more often than not ready to accept people. They must have felt safe with Toni. I think it's only when women feel threatened that we react out of fear.

"Everyone's seen Les Girls, it's great fun, a beaut night out. You must come," I was urged by a friend. That was back in the 1960s. I was a young mother and I confess now that I definitely did not want to go. I wasn't a party person and would have preferred a quiet evening at home watching the 'telly' or snuggled up reading a book.

Nevertheless, I was persuaded, and with a certain degree of trepidation went with Richard and a group of work-mates to a performance of the popular show-girls at a St. Kilda club near the foreshore.

With the risk of upsetting any of the 'girls' who were in the show, and who might read this chapter, I just couldn't seem to get the point – no pun intended – to the show. Why would a mob of blokes put on glitzy, girly costumes, kick their legs and prance around the stage, miming a few popular songs? Mind you, some of them could dance very well. It just wasn't my choice of entertainment. Now if they had actually sung their own songs, I may have been more impressed. One aspect that I couldn't seem to make sense of, was why on earth did they have men dressed as women? How come they didn't employ 'real' girls? I just didn't get it! But I confess I was very curious about what they did with 'it'? (Now I know how they conceal their genitals, but some confidences between a mother and child are best kept!)

Edna Everage, some years later, so popular and in vogue was so close to the bone in her observations that I was too wary of her scathing type of performance to actually enjoy her talent. As an older woman, I can now appreciate her skill and her humour and she doesn't frighten me any more. Edna is in a class of her own and I can't reconcile her as anything like the Les Girls showgirls that I watched perform all those years ago.

So with my naïve background and limited former experiences behind me I was scared and reluctant about going along when Toni invited the family to see a performance of a brand new show in town. A female impersonator, who Toni assured me would be a marvellous performer, was heading a cast of show-girls. I suspect he was attempting to resurrect a new, 1990s style show in the style of Les Girls. As well, Toni knew one or two of the chorus girls, so was really keen for us to watch them with her. 'It'll be a great night, Mum. You'll see.'

I hid my nervous anxiety about going to a nightclub and persuaded Richard to come along. My hope was that by exposing ourselves to more exotic and different people we would help ourselves to accept diversity, while hopefully having a good night out and we would keep Toni company and cheer her up.

The star performed acceptably well, mimed, danced and told a few jokes. Actually, I found him to be a much better comedian than anything else. Perhaps this was because my ideas were so firmly entrenched from my staid upbringing. I felt uncomfortable and I noticed Andrew drinking more than one or two bourbon and cokes. Maybe I should have had a couple more glasses of wine, but I'm telling it like it was and truth is I couldn't wait for the show to finish.

When Toni suggested a movie, that was a different matter entirely. I love the cinema and was looking forward to viewing the film Toni wanted to see about a transsexual woman living in London. Though it was still early days in our outings with our new daughter, we wanted to support her. Richard found it a bit confronting, but eventually agreed to come along, so Toni, Andrew, Richard and I went in to the art-house movie theatre and I for one thoroughly enjoyed the film. And it was good to watch a story unfold about a transsexual woman's experiences trying to blend into the work force and about her romantic attachment which eventually disintegrated due to the problem the boyfriend had in fully accepting her as she was.

My senses were constantly alert in those early days and as the lights dimmed I noticed a 'woman' wearing full length dark-coloured garments and a long wig topped by a floppy felt hat sneak into a side seat in front of us. She was very tall and somehow seemed so alone. When the movie was almost finished she crept out of the cinema before the lights came up again.

Afterwards I noticed the same 'woman' browsing at a bookstall near the front of the theatre and I was able to observe her in full light. Again I noticed how very sad she seemed; so sad I could almost touch her pain. I wished I had the courage to say 'Hi' or at least to spare a smile. These days I could. I know I can't do anything to ease another's pain, but a smile couldn't have hurt.

Several months passed before Toni again suggested a movie.

'Ma Vie en Rose', a film about the childhood and growing up of a young transsexual male to female, was showing at the art theatres and Toni had a new friend she wanted me to meet. By then I was ready to meet more of Toni's girlfriends and looked forward to both meeting the friend and going out to another movie. Richard was still having a bit of trouble going out in public with Toni, so this time he declined.

Both Toni and her friend were quite emotionally affected by the story as it unfolded on the big screen. They felt it was in many ways very close to their own experiences and it brought back memories of how they had felt during their childhood and particularly the difficult times of their adolescence. Toni didn't invite me to any more shows, as by then she and I were ready to pursue our own entertainment paths.

15

Close Encounters of the Sexual Kind

There are men who are attracted to 'chicks with dicks'. This information came as an absolute revelation to me. My knowledge of the nightclub scene, second-hand though it was, was widening mostly via Toni's stories about her experiences. Often I didn't really want to know some things, but nevertheless I was told. And so I learnt about 'tran-fans' when Toni's friends offered friendly warnings about them.

Some guys simply found transsexual women fascinating and my opinion is they might be attracted by the fact that transsexual people know what it's like to live on both sides of the fence. Maybe some of those 'tran-fan' men were sitting right on the top of the palings themselves. Were they envious, I wondered?

I don't know, but I heard about a few less than savoury characters as well, the 'tran-fags', which I think refers to men who can't openly admit their homosexuality so prefer to have relationships with a transsexual woman. This tag also belongs to men who abuse transsexual women because they are so vulnerable and they take advantage of the transsexuals' weaknesses.

By the time Toni was beginning to venture out alone at night she was under the wing of the 'mother hen'. I gave this lovely lady a nickname and I believe she is well aware that I'm not the only one who refers to her occasionally by this well earned and well meant title. This woman cares for all transsexual people and supports them in whatever way she is able to. So 'mother hen' also told Toni to be wary in her relationships with men.

As a concerned mother it was exceedingly difficult to come to terms with the knowledge that Toni was now going out alone. There was nothing I could do but pray for her safety and do my best not to worry.

All along this diverse path I was now travelling, Toni was always open with me. As I have inferred previously, often far too wide open for my peace of mind. Accepting her new friends, the world she was exposing herself to and the possibility of real danger was a secondary part of my process of growth, as I acquired knowledge of an area previously beyond my ken.

Where Toni's sexual preference might lie she was totally honest about and she told me. "I don't know what I'll end up, Mum. At present I am totally celibate and that's the way I want to be until I can accept a man when I'm physically more like a whole woman when I've had my surgery." Once she went so far to be even more blunt and crude. "My arse is for pooing not for screwing." From memory she blurted out that phrase when she was angry that someone had suggested she might be homosexual.

Although Toni had gay friends too and was totally tolerant of their sexuality that wasn't her particular choice. Eventually she wanted to have vaginal sex with a man and she said that she was prepared to wait.

This was the way Toni thought her sexuality would most likely lie in the future but she confided that things might change. She was confused about whether she would always feel this way or whether she might become a lesbian woman. These matters she was prepared to wait for and allow them to evolve with the course of time.

However it wasn't long before Toni coped with an incident involving a 'tran-fag'.

She'd been to a nightclub where she had met a man a couple of times. She was attracted to his nice smile, good looks and pleasant conversation. He bought a few drinks and they enjoyed chatting together. After a while he began to become more familiar, but not until after he'd flattered Toni with all of the words she wanted to hear, like how beautiful she was, what a slim and divine figure she possessed and so on.

As I heard a few days later when Toni confided the full story, the man's name was André. He said he was a famous artist, with a portrait-winning painting in one of Australia's most prestigious portrait painting competitions. I never actually learnt what this man's surname was and I don't know that Toni ever knew his full name herself. 'I want to paint you too, Toni. You're gorgeous.' The man hinted at his wealth and his world of travel, famous people and mixing with other rich and fascinating folk in the art world. Then he invited Toni to dinner. So off they went to the casino, where they ate a delicious meal of crustacean followed by sitting at the tables for an hour or two of roulette.

Now I do not want to give the impression that Toni was totally gullible. She is not. However, she was at that time in her life ready for new experiences and possibly just a little too eager to believe whatever she was told. Although she was cautious of André and not sure how much of what he said was truth, she wanted to enjoy herself with a man and the night on the town was going well. They were both having a great time and not yet ready to have the evening end.

"Let's call in to McDonald's for supper," André suggested. Toni was by then driving her own car. Previously they had used taxis to get to the nightclub and the casino and now the night was drawing to a close they had gone back to pick up her car from where the evening had begun. She wondered briefly how come André didn't have his own car, but thought it must be because he was concerned about drink-driving. Anyway as it turned out, lucky for Toni she had her own transport.

So they stopped for a hamburger and you guessed it, coffee at his place, except that it was his sister's apartment. Alarm bells began to ring. But Toni had consumed enough alcohol to relax her judgement and so off she went with him.

Toni insisted on only a cup of coffee because she knew she needed to sober up a bit before driving home. André showed her some of his paintings and Toni began to realise that at least part of what he had told her about himself was true. He really was an artist – and a good one at that. Maybe he was rich, but why was he living in his sister's apartment that was less than salubrious?

At this point in her story, Toni became visibly upset and I sure as anything didn't really want to know what happened next but she was hell-bent on telling me all of the details.

"I came to, wearing a red nightie. I had no memory of undressing or being dressed in something else. I felt groggy and knew I'd been slipped something in my coffee. Then I realised André was trying to stick his cock in my mouth."

I shuddered, wishing Toni could confide in someone else, but she continued.

"He had a scarf around my neck and I knew I was in real trouble, Mum."

Toni proceeded to tell me about how she quickly recovered her senses. Danger had sobered her clouded mind and self-preservation took over.

"I'm still bigger and stronger than he was, Mum. He was on top of me, but I managed to get my knee up and gave him an almighty kick in the 'cods'. I got outside and realised I was wearing nothing but that nightie. I didn't fancy running to the car wearing so little, and besides my handbag was still in the flat with my car keys in it on so I was forced to go back. Scared, but now knowing I was able to take care of myself, I knocked on the door and I demanded that he give me back my clothes and my bag. He passed them to me like a lamb and begged my forgiveness. I got dressed and kissed him goodbye."

I knew Toni meant that she 'kissed' him figuratively and not literally. Well anyway I hope that's what she meant.

I tried to persuade Toni to take the matter further and make a police report, but she wouldn't. This example proved to me, as if I needed any proof, that these girls are wide open to abuse by men who have few morals and that they take their life into their hands very often, so ready are they to hear sweet words. One thing, Toni learnt early on that she must be more careful and she was.

When I heard the story about Toni and the artist I noticed the particular male-type word that she had used for 'penis' and a couple of days later, when she had recovered from her experience, I spoke to her about it.

As Toni was doing her best to study the female voice, which involved much more than simply a higher pitch, I knew she would want to know my opinion to help her sound more female. Women use different speech patterns, but there are also words which males use and a female usually would not, so I told her, "Toni, a woman wouldn't use that word, perhaps they might say 'dick' instead." If one of my sons had used the word 'cock' I knew they would not say it in my presence, so it had come as a shock to hear Toni use that word. She was grateful and asked if I noticed her using the 'wrong type' of speech to please help her. I never did again, but that was one word I thought sounded too crude for a lady to use.

Next time a man came along, she waited until she had got to know him much better. She told me about a Scottish guy with a very strong brogue, and all about the fact that he lived with another transsexual woman. This man was struggling with his relationship. It was turning sour and it was the typical, 'She doesn't understand me,' story.

"God, Toni, don't get sucked in by this guy." I urged. "He'll lead you up the garden path. And are you ready to be involved with a two-timer?"

Well, it seemed like she was. For a little while she met this man for dinner or coffee or sometimes at a nightclub. When she felt sure that he was a gentle giant and he wasn't likely to take advantage of her, she made again another mistake. She wouldn't put herself in the position of meeting a man in his own home, but by then Toni wasn't living with us and she invited him to visit at her home. Andrew lived there as well and she felt safe with this man. But she wasn't ready for a sexual relationship. That would come later, after surgery. Well as it turned out, this man, although he had been told of Toni's celibacy, obviously didn't believe her. His first visit ended abruptly when he discovered she was serious about her sex life remaining chaste; another lesson in life for Toni about men. You would think she would have had enough with the André episode, but there was quite a way to go yet for Toni in her relationships with men.

16

Worrisome Whiskers

Whenever Toni was preparing herself with make-up, hairdo and dress she looked to the family for approval, but mostly it was me, her mother, she asked whether she would 'pass' or not. In the early months, Toni was consumed by concern over her facial hair.

Packets and packets of razor blades were used. Her 'Epi-Lady' hair removing machine got maximum use and waxes and depilatories were all experimented with. For bodily hair all of these measures were fine and once Toni began hormone treatment much of her hair growth slowed. Amazingly, hormones work in an opposite way for hair on the head. 'Bum-fluff' began to grow on the baldy patches and at first I thought Toni was imagining the new growth. But soon I could see the emerging tiny tufts of hair. Toni was ecstatic about the new hair growth on her head.

Unfortunately, facial hair is a much more difficult growth to control. Once puberty has passed and male growth has well and truly established itself on the face, nothing much worked. There was some softening and lessening of growth due to the hormones, but not sufficient. What would she do?

Again technology was a help via the internet. Toni was still establishing herself among new friends and hadn't yet come to rely on them. She searched the Yellow Pages for laser treatment and decided this was probably the only almost permanent way to go. The other possibility was electrolysis, but that method was simply too slow for Toni's requirements.

The trouble with laser treatment was the cost. So Toni worked hard at the business and saved every cent she could towards the day she could afford to begin to be rid of her 'whiskers'.

Recalling Tony's adolescence, I had no knowledge of how difficult that time of his life must have been for him. I was proud to see him maturing and the normal type of bodily changes occurring to his male body. Little did I know that those whiskers sprouting were such a pain for him to bear; only now since Toni has told me about the hard time he was suffering at school and during his childhood do I realise some of what went on.

Once, years later, when Tony was a young married man, I remember him discussing the possibility of electrolysis treatment for his beard. It all seemed to me to be such a silly notion. "Buy why, Tony? What on earth would you want to go to all that expense for?" He shrugged off the expense and said it would be worth it. Then he added that he was sick of shaving, as some sort of explanation to me, I suppose. Now, as I think of some of the unusual little things that happened, the jig-saw puzzle begins to fit together.

Apparently Tony lived through years of bullying during adolescence, none of which I was aware was happening. If ever my children complained to me of bullying, I would have said, "Sticks and stones will break your bones, names will never hurt you," and advise them to turn the other cheek and the bully would soon get sick of their behaviour if they received no pleasure from it. But little did I know how much Tony was putting up with. And sometimes, he tells me now, there was more than verbal abuse. Many a time he was accused of being a 'sissy', 'girly' or 'weird'. Certainly Tony's appearance was never effeminate, but children are often wiser than adults and they had perceived that Tony was unusual in some way.

Yet another clue that puzzled me at the time, was again an incident that happened when Tony was a young married man. The incident related to his eyebrows. Tony and his wife had come to visit for the Christmas period and I noticed most of his eyebrows were missing. This seemed more than a little perplexing, especially since neither Tony nor Judith seemed to offer any convincing explanation over what had caused his eye-brows to suddenly become so thin. What had actually been done to the eyebrows was that Tony had plucked them all into a thin line.

These days I would not dare refer to Toni's 'facial hair' as whiskers. Women don't grow whiskers. But lots of ladies have some hair growth on their face. Perhaps as I grow a little older I may be tempted to try laser on one or two hormonal hairs myself.

So it happened that the first Christmas Toni was with our family, Richard and I gave her a voucher for her first consultation with a laser treatment salon. Never, ever, could I possibly have imagined a more unusual gift to be presenting to one of my children!

After much searching and visits to various salons to find a place where she would feel comfortable she went along for her first visit, but dressed as Tony. She was afraid of how she might be treated if she turned up for her first treatment as Toni.

By the time Toni was having her third or fourth treatment, she realised that the staff had worked out that Toni was a transsexual woman and had treated a few others just like her. So from then on she went for her treatment in female garb.

One thing Toni hated about the laser treatment, was not the fact that it stung a bit – 'like elastic bands hitting your face' – or the fact that her skin was red and sore for a couple of days. None of that meant a thing to Toni, as long as she was getting rid of the dreaded growth. And Toni was fortunate that she had dark, strong whiskers that were easy to be rid of by laser treatment. What Toni dreaded more than anything else was that firstly she couldn't shave for a few days prior to treatment. Her facial hair must be long enough for the laser to attack. Secondly she was not supposed to wear make-up for a couple of days after treatment. Toni fairly soon ignored that particular suggestion and covered up the redness with foundation.

Between treatments whenever a stray hair popped up, tweezers were used to pluck out the offending little blighters. How often Toni inquired as to whether I could notice any growth, I could not count, but be assured it was frequently. By the time Toni had completed several visits to the laser ladies, facial hair became less and less of a problem. How glad I was that those worrisome whiskers were almost obliterated. In the future an occasional treatment should be all that will be required to eliminate any small stray hairs. Thank God for that!

17

Officially Toni

One of the requirements of people accepted for assessment with the gender reassignment team is that they must live full-time for a period of approximately two years before they will be accepted for surgery. Some people have lived full-time for many, many years prior to when they first began to seek treatment. Among many other things that the doctors take into consideration is that these people must be deemed capable of coping with life as a person living in the opposite role to their birth body.

From Toni's first appointment with the team she began attempting to live always as Toni. This was not quite possible for a little while as she had her livelihood to consider. There had not been time yet to come out to her customers. So for a few weeks she cheated a bit and if she had to, she donned Tony's clothes when she had work related visits. Toni was afraid she might lose too much business if she tried to introduce Toni too soon or to too many people at once.

She began to answer the phone pretending to be Tony's secretary, just to see if she could get away with her new voice. Sometimes clients picked Tony and asked what was wrong with his voice, did he have a cold or something? Gradually though, her voice became accepted and clients sometimes asked to speak to her boss. That posed another difficulty. Should Toni fob them off and say the boss was out or revert back to her Tony voice. On more than one or two occasions she had to do that because there was business to discuss that the secretary would not have been able to cope with. Of course this was a real Jekyll-and-Hyde life-style and one that did not at all appeal to Toni. She only wanted to be Toni.

'I'm going to come-out to my customers, Mum" Toni told me. "I can't keep on living a charade. Besides they'll have to find out sooner or later."

Afraid that her business would suffer drastically, but knowing that what she said was the truth, I kept quiet and nodded in agreement. I knew this would be a testing time for everyone. Up until that time, Andrew had been running in to business places, picking up or dropping off orders and generally doing what he could for Toni both because he was now a working partner in the business, but also to spare Toni embarrassment. Increasingly this became impossible because Andrew did not yet have sufficient knowledge about the business to always be able to make those visits. Sometimes Tony was required to see someone and was forced to present in his male clothing.

Often I would hear Toni's conversations with clients, because the 'office' was situated in a corner of our family room, so it was impossible for me not to overhear. But when Toni decided to let clients know what was going on, she mostly found a time when I wasn't around or she went in to her bedroom to make the calls more private. I was grateful for her consideration.

But there were one or two occasions when I did hear the one-sided telephone conversation of Toni's coming-out and I confess I found the long gaps and silences quite amusing. I conjured up pictures of the people's faces on the other end of the line.

Some clients couldn't have cared less about what Tony was now, as long as they were assured their jobs would still be out to them on time and be of the same high quality that they had come to expect from the business.

There were a couple of people who said they'd already

worked out something like this was happening by Toni's voice and so were glad to know that their imagination had not been working over-time. They just accepted the new situation and continued to submit orders.

Still others were accepting but totally curious. Toni spent several long-distance extended telephone calls to those clients, telling them all about the process her personal life was undergoing and about the reasons for her change. They wanted details and Toni was more than happy to talk to anyone who would listen, glad to at last be able to discuss these matters with others.

Unfortunately there are people who cannot accept 'different' people and they can be extremely cruel. Bad luck for Toni that one of these people was in charge of a company for which she did a large volume of work.

Toni was wary of divulging much information to that particular client as she suspected he might be less than understanding. So for as long as possible she delayed any knowledge of her new life to this man. Eventually he heard from someone else, which probably didn't help the situation.

This company refused to give any further work to a person 'like that'. No matter how Toni tried to explain that they would receive the same product for the same price with no variation in quality they would not budge. Bigotry in this world is too widespread and often in the name of religion. This company was owned by a particular denomination that I will refrain from naming, but whom I thought would have been more charitable in their outlook. Not so! From that day no work came from them to the business.

At the time when Toni was revealing her female persona to her customers, she was starting to go through the lengthy process of procuring new documentation for identification purposes.

First step in acquiring her new identity meant a trip to the Office of Births, Deaths and Marriages in the city. All that was necessary was to part with a fee and they'd produce her former I.D – things such as her previous birth certificate, passport or other documents – in her present name.

Tony had chosen to just change the spelling of her first name. Her second given name was one that she selected with the same initial as the one she was given by Richard and myself when she was born. As Tony with a 'y' can be used for either sex she could have left it as was, but she needed to change her middle name as it was a purely male name, so she changed both first names officially by deed poll and became Toni Anna Langley.

She was given a certificate complete with her new name. However in Victoria it is not legally possible to alter 'Sex' on a birth certificate. Some states in Australia allow this to be done once surgery is complete, but not in Victoria. Seems this state still has some 'Victorian' attitudes.

T.L.C. are trying to lobby for the law in Victoria to be brought into line with the other States which already allow change of sex on a birth certificate, but so far with no luck. I see this as another example of confusing state laws in Australia. I feel there are many areas, perhaps especially road laws and education where I feel a standard throughout the country is long overdue. The change of sex on birth certificates for the transsexual population is surely a humanitarian need that must be addressed.

For Toni the possibility of being pulled over in her car and asked to produce her driver's licence was a fearful prospect. So she decided after deed poll was complete the first document that she would change must be her licence.

Luckily, as Toni only possessed a Western Australian driver's licence, which was not a photographic licence, she thought the process shouldn't be too confronting. Well it turned out to be somewhat more upsetting than she expected.

When she went to Vicroads where the system requires you to take a number and wait to be seen by the next available counter staff she was unfortunate enough to be seen by a man who immediately noticed her Western Australian drivers' licence bore the title 'Mr.'

"So you want a Victorian driver's licence, Sir?" the Vicroads employee asked with great emphasis on the 'Sir'. Toni tried to explain her situation, but this ignoramus was intent on ridiculing my daughter. He repeated the 'Mr' title loudly a few more times and refused to alter the licence without a fuss.

As usual the government office was filled with people attending each to their own business. By the time a few people had moved closer to see what was going on, their ears flapping, Toni could not cope. She grabbed her birth certificate and her deed poll papers with the rest of the necessary documentation and flounced out before obtaining her licence.

A woman working at the next computer appeared to be very sympathetic and was giving the man who caused Toni so much grief a few nasty looks. Encouraged by her apparent support, a few days later Toni returned and swapped numbers with other customers until she managed to be attended to by this lady.

Again armed with all the paperwork that was needed Toni quietly explained her need for a Victorian driver's licence, with a photo, which was mandatory anyway, and she wanted her title to be Ms on their records. The kindly Vicroads lady spent a long time attending to Toni's application and managed to find a way to achieve this on the computer; a task which took a little bit of technology side-stepping to erase her previous gender and add her new title.

A photograph of a smiling Toni now adorns her Victorian driver's licence. Hopefully she won't ever need to produce it for any driving misdemeanours but it is often required for identification purposes, and she is happy with her photo.

Once on a wet, wintry evening before she had changed to a Victorian licence, she was spoken to by a police officer who pulled up alongside her car. Toni was travelling home from the city alone and her mouth was dry and her palms wet. She held her breath wondering what she'd done and was nervous about her Western Australian licence, but the officer called her 'Ma'am' and didn't even ask to view her licence, just sent her on her way after advising her that her left-hand indicator was malfunctioning.

Next on the I.D. agenda was the bank, a much more difficult proposition. To this day she still finds her old name and title popping up from time to time. They simply refuse to delete her former gender.

I recall the day that a bank officer at the branch I use myself gave Toni a particularly hard time by laughing and making snide remarks about her to the next teller. This happened on several occasions. Eventually Toni decided to take a stand, so she rang the bank manager and complained. She threatened to proceed with anti-discrimination action if something wasn't done to rectify the situation and to ensure that she might complete her banking business in the future in a manner that did not cause her any further embarrassment. The manager wasn't entirely sympathetic, but Toni was persuasive because she knew her rights. He agreed to speak to the teller to make sure he stopped his discriminating behaviour.

By now I was defensive of my daughter's feelings and angry. Besides I had to be served on occasion by this particular young male teller, so I thought I would give him a little taste of his own medicine.

Next day I asked for his full name and let him think I was an officer from the anti-discrimination board, without actually saying that I was, and I gave him a few stern looks. Perhaps I shouldn't have done this, but I felt better afterwards, and combined with the warning that he must have received from his manager, he was always very polite to Toni when she did her banking.

Australia Post received a lot of custom from Toni's business as she posted most of her work to Perth. One day a particularly ignorant woman working behind the counter made loud remarks to another staff member that 'she didn't know if she was Arthur or Martha' with pointed looks in Toni's direction.

These incidents were extremely distressing for Toni and she often came home in tears when something like that happened. I advised her to keep going back to the same branch of Australia Post in the hope that once they got used to her appearance and knew they had nothing to fear, that she was in fact a very nice person, that things might change. And they did. Eventually they treated her kindly and no different to other customers.

Medicare files and other government papers, especially tax files, prove impossible to change. Details from the past keep popping up to annoy Toni.

As far as a passport is concerned Toni has had no need to update hers. If ever she wants to travel overseas she knows that her gender details can be altered on a new passport simply by producing a letter from her surgeon that confirms she has undergone gender reassignment surgery. This would make it safe for her to travel to countries where there could be a problem. A new passport would arrive with a letter attached stating that this passport cannot be used to alter her birth certificate in Victoria, but it would be issued for her with her gender stamped 'Female'.

18

Out of The Mouths of Babes

Our first Christmas with Toni in the family was only weeks away and I was madly shopping for gifts, especially for the children. Somehow we had survived a most challenging few months and I was looking forward to life settling down a little and to getting back some sort of normalcy. Just as well I didn't possess a crystal ball!

Again Mum had succumbed to pneumonia and she was this time a patient in the local Repatriation Hospital. Because I was expecting her to be discharged some time before Christmas, I felt an added pressure to complete my preparations for the festive season.

Mum had been through a very sick year, her health was still precarious and I realised she would need a bit extra care when she came home, so off I went to the shopping complex in search of toys.

With each gift that I purchased came a flashback of something that was connected with our recent past. For one thing, now I must purchase feminine gifts for my daughter instead of typical male socks and jocks or whatever I used to buy. When I picked up a 'fantasy house' for my youngest granddaughter, Katey, I recalled an incident that never fails to cause a smile to crinkle my lips.

The memory is of a day when my daughter-in-law was

unable to do her 'fruit duty' at the kindergarten, so Paul did his fatherly bit and went in her place.

The four-year old children were busy painting pictures of families on white butcher's paper. Paul was standing beside Katey's easel admiring her artwork when the teacher stopped next to them. She asked Katey about her painting. When Katey pointed to a tall image of 'Uncle' Toni the teacher, surprised but with no knowledge of what her comment meant to Paul and Katey, remarked, "But Katey, men don't wear dresses." Quick as only a child can be, she retorted indignantly, "Oh yes they do!" with great emphasis on the word 'do'.

I realised how very accepting children can be of the transformation of a human being from one form to another, but on the other hand I was annoyed with the teacher. Of course most men don't wear dresses, but what about male Fijians in their sarongs or the Scot in his kilt or the tall, regal Masai warrior?

Little did the teacher know of our transsexual family member, though Paul told me he felt the colour rise in his cheeks and that day he was very glad when his kindergarten duty was over.

Gradually the children in our family chose, with a little encouragement from their parents, to address Toni as 'Aunty'. Surprisingly they adjusted quickly and Aunty Toni she was.

What we tell the kids had been an unspoken question in my mind because I knew it wouldn't be up to me. Their parents must decide when, where and how much to tell them. All the children in the family were either pre-school or in their first year or two of school, which proved an easier prospect than if they'd been older. Well, I think so. Young children are so resilient and mostly, fairly non-judgemental.

Paul and Mary told me they simply told their girls that there are some men who would like to be women and that from now on they would see Uncle Tony wearing female clothing. Paul did speak to Tony in the early days when he wasn't always wearing female clothes and he asked that he make sure that when the children were coming Toni be consistent. Now that they had seen Toni, could she please present that way all the time and not dress in male clothing again when they were there, so that the children would not be confused.

Paul was having a difficult time accepting the situation himself and was finding it difficult to address his 'brother' as 'she'. Andrew had spent so much more time with Toni that his acceptance was much further advanced than was Paul's.

As head of the family Richard took it upon himself to correct Paul once or twice and Richard attempted to always use the feminine pronouns himself; a task which proved beyond him for a little while longer, but he was trying very hard.

It was tough for us all, but not as hard as it must have been for Toni. She became so angry whenever we slipped up and said 'he'. I shed many tears over the he/she words. They became my bugbear. As a mother accustomed for more than thirty-five years to calling her off-spring 'he' to suddenly have to say 'she' was confusing beyond belief.

One day I had had enough of Toni's prima donna antics when once again I had uttered the male pronoun, so I let her have it and told her that we were doing our very best to adjust, but that our 'computers' weren't so easy to alter. On occasion my brain and mouth simply refused to compute 'she' with Toni. So I told her she would have to like it or lump it. I was doing my best and that would just have to be good enough. I was sure that eventually we could get used to the new pronouns, but for now we were doing the best that we could manage.

My anger was paramount when Toni called his grandmother, 'grandpa' in an attempt to force her into changing her pronouns when speaking about her. I explained that given her grandmother's age and state of health she was marvellously accepting and loving towards her. And she was more than generous – often purchasing small feminine gifts for Toni.

Sometimes I found myself repeating the phrase to Toni,

'Actions speak louder than words' – a cliché that was being actively lived in our household. I reminded her that she was living with us and how lucky she was to have family support.

I finished the Christmas shopping and was glad to pack my reminiscences away as I wrapped each gift for the family and placed them under the tree. A card for my father was ready to be posted and this disturbed my satisfaction that I had completed my task that day. Sadly I knew that this would probably be my father's last Christmas. Maybe he might not even be with us this year because his bowel cancer had advanced and was now in his liver. I licked the envelope and kissed the back of it before popping it in the mail, praying that he was not suffering too badly.

19

Second Coming Out

"Simon's been killed."

Those words immediately flung me back thirty-four years to a wet winter night when Richard's father came to my door and snapped that very same sentence.

On that evening, so long ago, my father-in-law's appearance reminded me of a scarecrow, his arms were all over the place and his wide eyes seemed as if they were stitched open. His lips, set in a grim straight line, could have been glued to his face.

Richard's brother had been killed at work. A pulley belt on one of the factory machines had broken and Simon had been caught then dragged into the machine by his left arm. His injuries were immediately fatal. Simon was just fourteen years old.

Now his namesake the young man who would have been Simon's nephew, had also met a violent death. This time we heard the news by telephone in the middle of a warm summer night two weeks before Christmas, 1997.

Richard's youngest brother gave him a sketchy outline of what had happened. Simon had been trying to get a lift in a stranger's car near the busy intersection on a stretch of a main northbound road, for some reason unknown to them. He had somehow been dragged along the road by a car and had suffered fatal head injuries.

Woken from our sleep, this all seemed like another terrible nightmare. But it wasn't. Quickly we donned the nearest clothes we could find and drove to my mother-in-law's home. Simon's parents and some of the rest of the family were gathered there because her home was less than half a kilometre from the public hospital where Simon had been taken.

Morning light was beginning to break over the hill, and we could see the outline of the hospital's chimney-stack and knew that Simon was probably still in there. This was the very same hospital where Toni was born, so I knew it very well. For a moment I drifted back in time to a couple of visits we'd made to the emergency department, once when Toni was a tiny baby suffering colic which caused him to cry mercilessly for hours on end. No matter how we tried to soothe him, still he cried. Thinking he must be ill with something worse, we had taken him to the emergency department.

It's amazing how much you can think about in a ten-minute car ride. Richard and I were mostly lost in our own thoughts, though we wondered out loud what on earth had happened and what were the circumstances of Simon's death. We talked about his deceased brother Simon as well. What we didn't discuss was Richard's sister, Helen and her husband, Kevin. We could only imagine what their grief must be like and we didn't want to confront that until we had to.

When we arrived Helen's eyes were swollen and red but they were dry. We hugged briefly and once again her tears flowed. What I remember about her grief, more than anything else, was the way her mouth quivered and how her bottom lip was curled over in a continuous kind of movement, like a rocking motion – as if that might comfort her in some way. Anger was the next emotion that became evident. She was angry with everyone, including her son who had just been killed. Helen's grief was too painful to watch, but watch it we did.

Our children had been babies and toddlers together.

Many a Sunday roast we had shared with our little ones in this tiny kitchen, more suited to a retired couple than a large extended family. How many happy and how many sad times that room had witnessed. If only the walls could speak, I wouldn't need to write this book.

Kevin was there too and he was equally upset, but there was a bond between us two sisters-in-law that gave me more insight to a mother's grief than his. Richard went outside with his brother-in-law for a while and they talked 'man-talk' and he tried to comfort him.

The story that Helen told us was what she knew at that stage. Simon had been to a cricket team Christmas party break-up; he had called his fiancee and she had come to collect him. On the way home for some reason, he had decided he wanted to get out of the car, perhaps to return to the party. Anyway, his fiancee had no alternative but to let him go his own way. In doing so he had tried to get into someone's car, apparently to ask for a lift, and somehow had been dragged along the road by this car, maybe run over. We didn't know exactly what had happened.

There was nothing we could do to ease the grief of my sister-in-law and brother-in-law. We were hurting ourselves; we had just lost a dearly loved nephew. I felt helpless. So we returned home and spent a quiet, reflective day with our own immediate family. My unspoken grief at losing my own son – though he was not physically dead, to me he was just as dead as Simon – was causing me extra sadness, particularly as no-one else even knew what I was thinking, let alone how I was feeling. And I felt there was no one in the world, except perhaps Richard, who could begin to understand my confused grief.

Once much later, when my sister-in-law and I were talking together about her son and how very sad she still was, and the fact that she didn't feel like living herself, I confided in her what I was feeling. She pointed out that I had Toni, a new daughter to hold and to hug, while she could never touch her son again. I knew I had my daughter, Toni, and I love her very much. That wasn't the point in question. It was as though having lost one of a whole brood you still mourn the one that is missing. Whether or not there be a dozen others left, my eldest son is missing.

During the previous week, my sister had rung me from Sydney with the news that my father's liver cancer had progressed and he wasn't expected to live much longer. As Dad lived in Bendigo, we had arranged to meet there the following Sunday.

By then Dad had been admitted to the hospice part of the country hospital.

Simon died on Saturday night and we were exhausted by the time we returned home. This was on the morning we were supposed to take the long drive to Bendigo. So we rang my sister, who by then had arrived in Bendigo, and decided we would go on Monday, which we did.

Dad was conscious and appeared to be resting quite comfortably when I saw him. I took him some stalks of lavender from the front garden of his home, hoping the smell would evoke recognition. He knew who I was anyway, there was still nothing wrong with his marvellous mind and he chided me about bringing lavender. "I'm sick of the stuff," he said. "I'm forever cutting it back, away from the front path." Then he drifted off again, sleeping for a while. When he woke I asked him about his pain. He assured me he was not suffering, a sentiment he had been telling anyone who visited him, insisting, "I do not have any pain."

The hospice staff was amazed. They had treated many patients with terminal liver cancer. It wasn't that they thought my father was lying. They said that he must have pain, yet if he did he was controlling it himself without the aid of any strong medication. All his life he had believed in natural therapy and he refused morphine. I talked to Dad, begging him not to try and be brave and to accept whatever pain relief he required. He just told me he didn't need any morphine, that he had conceded to taking *two* Panadol tablets, something he had never done in his life. So maybe, that was enough to help him or perhaps his will power was stronger than pain.

Although my visit was sad, it was not tragic. My good-byes were said with a few tears and with much love. Dad was seventy-seven years old and had lived a good life.

He always said he would live to be one hundred. That was one aspect of my sadness. I knew he wasn't going to make his century.

Tuesday afternoon brought another kind of news, again a tragic telephone call, this time with a message delivered by my mother-in-law. "Simon was shot. There's a bullet in his head."

Following the 'road accident', Simon had been transferred to the Coroner's Office for an autopsy. In hindsight, the hospital staff may already have known about the bullet wound, though I'm not sure about that, or even whether his head was X-rayed while he was in the Emergency Department of the hospital, because by the time he arrived there I think he was already dead. The police had rung and spoken to my brother-in-law at their home. My mother-in-law was there with them, when they received the call. She told me that Kevin screamed and threw the telephone across the room in shock. His son had been murdered.

This awful complication would mean a delay of several more days before Simon's funeral arrangements could be finalised. Eventually, almost a week later, the funeral was scheduled to be held in a large Catholic church, close to their home. The burial was to be in the grounds of a peaceful lawn cemetery where his body would be laid to rest.

As Christmas was only a few days away, Toni and Andrew were rushing to complete orders and they hoped that the Christmas mail would not delay their delivery. Consequently Toni did not have time to worry about going out to get something to wear to the funeral. But she did have time to think about it and she was very concerned about what was appropriate to wear. After all she'd only been 'dressing' full-time for a couple of months and her female clothing was either too casual or suitable only for nightclubs.

I agreed to look for an outfit for Toni at the local op-shop. She did not have much money to spend and besides I didn't want to get an expensive suit that may not fit. Toni has long arms and is tall; her back and shoulders are a little broader than a woman's average size 14, but I felt sure I would probably find something to fit at the local Salvation Army shop.

There I discovered a designer-label two piece suit, deep lavender in colour with a tiny print, that looked long enough in the sleeves and long enough in the skirt to fit her. It was a beautiful outfit and cost only a few dollars.

The day before the funeral I began to be consumed by conflicting feelings. I was so sad because of what had happened to my nephew, but I was also worried about my daughter's 'coming out' to more of the family. Up until then, of course all of our immediate and most of our extended family knew all about Toni and were comfortable enough with her. I was thinking about some of the rest of the family whom I cared about, who had not yet been told and I was wishing we had let them know earlier. So I rang Richard's cousin and explained what had been going on in our household over the previous months. They were absolutely marvellous and assured me of their support. The cousin I had rung agreed to let her sisters know before the funeral the next day. Any other members of the extended family would see Toni on the day and find out that way. I really didn't care too much about whether they would be accepting or not.

Both of the major newspapers, television and radio stations had been full of news about Simon's accident, then as it turned out, his murder. The situation was unusual, so it was very newsworthy. I expected the funeral would be a large one and I knew there would be reporters and photographers present.

We all needed a good sleep in preparation for the big day ahead of us. I knew I would have to be there and be strong. The day would be difficult for me but I must support my daughter, my sister-in-law and her family and most of all to be there at the sad farewell to my nephew.

My sleep was restless anyway, as I tossed around thoughts about everything that had happened and my fears about Toni's coming out at such a large family funeral were worrying me. I knew that everyone would be there because of Simon's death and that would be their paramount concern, so I tried desperately to put aside any thoughts about people who might be tempted to sneak a second look at Toni. I must be tough and remembered that I was growing a thick outer skin that was a necessity for me now.

When I finally drifted into a deeper sleep the telephone woke me. I thought at first I was dreaming, and when I took the call I wished that I had been. "Dad passed away half an hour ago, Lyn." It was my sister ringing from Bendigo with the sad news. I wept for my father. I wept for Simon and for his mother and the rest of the family. I wept for my grief about Tony and I wept for myself.

By the time we got to the funeral, I had few tears left. Toni looked beautiful. She wore the newer, longer wig, which was an auburn shade, different from her own very dark brown hair. Toni's make-up was a little too heavily applied for my liking; nevertheless, she was quite lovely. Her nails were long and carefully manicured and painted to match the colour of her suit, and her accessories were matched – all black. However, because it was still early days in her transformation she looked different enough that some people could still 'read' her. To me, her mother, I was very aware of how she was before, so she still appeared not to 'pass' totally. Looking back, I realise a lot of the time I took more notice than anyone else did.

The cousins I had told the previous day were true to their word. They sat in the pews behind us and offered many a quiet touch and a loving hand to hold. They stayed close by our family and supported us.

Unfortunately my fears about curious looks from other members of the congregation were well-founded. There were one or two among the more than one thousand mourners who were from our more distant family and they seemed to be more interested in looking at Toni than being there for the purpose of the day. I tried to disregard their curious stares.

Dad's funeral was held three days later in a quiet Bendigo chapel. The service was conducted by an elderly friend of my father's, a retired clergyman. Wreaths of native flowers adorned his coffin and I knew Dad would have loved them. The day was a celebration of his life and in stark contrast to the tragic funeral of a young man who died too soon, a few days earlier.

Once again I had been forced to reveal Toni's new identity. This was not the ideal time to have to tell my step-mother such unusual news, but she was amazingly compassionate and understanding. I told her that her husband's grandson would not be at the funeral. In his place would be Toni, a granddaughter my father had never met. I regret that I had not been able to tell Dad about her. I know he would have been accepting and I keep that in my mind whenever I struggle with my own acceptance.

20

Burying a Lemon

The Queen of England named a particularly bad year for her an 'annus horribilis'.

1997 was most definitely mine, and it was one that I wished to put behind me. My aim was to move on with my life and to make 1998 a new beginning.

Part of my process in moving forward was aided by role models and heroes. They were sometimes people whom I had never met. As a mother I empathised with the Queen of England and she became one of those role models. Her family had caused her much anguish, yet she continued to perform her royal duties under the watchful eye of a very critical public. All of her children's woes were much publicised in the world's media. Absolutely nothing escaped its eagle eye. The paparazzi followed them unmercifully.

I was determined to follow the role model of a woman from the northern antipodes and in so many aspects another world away from my own problems. Her British stiff upper lip was something I had needed to emulate during those first difficult months during 1997.

Christmas had come and gone. We'd spent Christmas day with Caitlin, my niece, at her apartment by the sea. It was a beautiful sunny day and we were determined to make the most of the celebration. This year was a departure from how our family usually spent the day. I normally cooked the traditional hot roast turkey, pork, ham and all of the roast vegetables and trimmings, followed by the obligatory plum pudding and custard. The day was spent at home. So this was the first time in many, many years when I was to be served a meal not cooked by myself and I was unbelievably grateful to my young niece.

With my father's funeral only three days earlier and Simon's three days prior to his, I can't pretend that it was the happiest of days. But I did my best to put my grief aside for the day. When we all sat at one long table, seated with many of Caitlin's friends and her partner's family, it felt so unusual and different. This thought reminded me that my life would never, ever be the same again and that I had just better adjust to it the way it was and get on with things in a new way.

As is traditional in so many family gatherings on this day, our first bit of fun was to attack the bon-bons and crack them open, put on the silly party hats, blow the paper whistles and then read all the inane jokes from the centre of the crackers. My eyes could scarcely believe the content of the joke that I had discovered inside my cracker. I read it and the irony of finding that particular joke inside my bon-bon still causes me to gasp. I read the joke to our immediate family, all seated around me.

It went like this … Question: Do robots have brothers?

Answer: No, only transisters.

Well, we certainly had a tran-sister in our family now and we laughed long and hard, all of us struck by the odds of us being the ones with this joke inside our Christmas cracker. I believe it was a message to me to lighten up and I did.

The extended family was loving and thoughtful in their choice of gifts for Toni. Almost everyone gave her things like perfume, make-up, a pretty T-shirt or some other feminine gift. One or two who found it difficult were nevertheless sensitive enough not to give her 'male' things and they chose unisex gifts such as a box of chocolates or a bottle of wine.

Toni was very happy that everyone had been so caring about her as the newest female member of the Langley family.

The other guests, many of whom we had not met before as they were Caitlin's boyfriend's family had obviously been 'worded-up' and they accepted Toni without exception and welcomed and included her in all the Christmas revelry. I couldn't help recognising that the true spirit of Christmas was that day alive and well at our celebratory table and I felt quite humbled by the experience.

During the days between Christmas and New Year I allowed myself time to spend in reflection on my father's life and from time to time disappeared into my bedroom when I felt too sad to be with anyone. I cried for my father. I had missed so much of the last twenty years of his life because of my parents' divorce. Dad had moved to Bendigo with his second wife not very long after she gave birth to a son. My half-brother had severe asthma and as they were living in the hills at that time, his doctor urged Dad to take the baby to a warmer climate, in the hope that his asthma would improve. From then on I saw my father only rarely and I missed him very much.

Now that he had gone forever, I was regretting the lost time. It was difficult to come to grips with that part of my grief, but fairly quickly I realised that I just needed to be grateful for the times we did spend together and I tried to focus on those good and happy memories.

A very dear friend had told me about an idea she'd heard about, burying a lemon when one had had a bad year. Then and there I decided that it might be a good idea for Richard and I to actually perform a short ceremony and physically carry out this act.

Toni and Andrew had gone out raging to one or several of their chosen nightclubs and I knew they would be having a great night together with their friends. Richard and I had been invited to a small party, but we declined. Mum was still too ill to go out and we had absolutely no wish to go to a party. In fact, I couldn't have gone if you'd paid me. Christmas had been something of an ordeal and I was determined that I wasn't going to force a happy face on New Year's Eve. I wanted to start afresh, but I was too sad to face a party.

In preparation for our evening together, we had bought some 'nibbles' and a bottle of champagne. We wouldn't miss out altogether; and we planned to watch the fireworks on Sydney Harbour on television and enjoy that. But not before we had done what we set out to do.

I had purchased the largest yellow lemon I could find in the supermarket. We used a black Texta pen and wrote '1997' on both sides of the lemon. Richard got a shovel out of the shed and with a steely look in his eye he set to work. He dug and he dug. "Hey, Richard, that'll do. It's deep enough," I told him. "No it's not. I'm going to bury that lemon as deep down as I can go," he replied. We tossed in the lemon and both shovelled the soil over it, wishing it goodbye and good riddance.

The ceremony was over and we found its value amazingly therapeutic. From now on, we decided, if life gives us lemons we'll make lemonade, but for that night the only way we could cope was to bury that particular lemon as deep as we could.

21

Shopping With the Girls

It was time for some retail therapy. The January sales were well under way and the whole family, except Andrew, who hates shopping, decided we would go out for a bit of a spending spree. Toni wanted to buy a soft, padded bra. Six months ago the idea that I would now be going to the lingerie department of Myer with her would have been laughable. Now it was my reality. I knew my extra skin, which by now was growing quite nicely, thank you very much, would come in very handy. The only way I could deal with some of my inner feelings was by slipping inside my elephant hide. If I pretended hard enough that I felt okay, then I suspected that eventually I really would feel fine as well.

Richard pushed Mum in her wheelchair, oxygen attached on the back, and I scurried forward with Toni. She always did walk quickly and today she was in a hurry to get what she wanted. We wandered around the racks, picking up lacy little numbers and we oohed and aahed over this one or that one. None of them were quite suitable for Toni. As she was broad across the back, yet small in front, she needed a size that was difficult to find. By then Richard had become embarrassed, not about Toni, but about hanging around women's underwear, so he disappeared with Mum.

I became aware of two women giggling together and imagined they had 'spotted' Toni. Probably they were enjoying a private joke, but I was so sensitive that I suffered a lot of unnecessary angst. My skin was softening. "Hurry up, Toni. I want to do some shopping too, you know." So we looked through the untidy sale racks and eventually found a bra that fitted. Well, we hoped it would. Toni didn't feel like going into the ladies' change room to try it on. She bought it and hoped for the best. Hormone treatment was only a few weeks along at that stage and actually Toni didn't have enough breast to fill a 'AA' cup. As long as it reached around her she could stuff it with whatever she used to fill her bras. I never actually asked her that question.

We met up with Richard and Mum and enjoyed a quiet cappuccino together. By now Richard had no qualms about venturing into public with Toni. She was his daughter and that was that. Anyone who gave them a hard time would have an irate father to deal with. Lucky for any curious starers that Richard takes little notice of whether people are looking or not. He goes his own way and is often oblivious to subtleties. Sometimes I wished I could be like him in that way. While we sipped our coffee Richard had us in stitches laughing about a recent incident at golf.

The guys at Richard's golf club had met Tony a couple of years previously and knew that Richard had three sons. Andrew also often played golf with the group his father had joined. They had played a round or two with Tony when he visited Melbourne for Christmas that year. As Richard began to tell his story, we urged him to hurry up. He has a knack of taking a long time to get to the punch line and we thought this was a joke that he was telling us.

"You've got three sons, haven't you Richard?" his golfing buddy asked.

"Well I used to have three sons," Richard replied. "Now I've got two sons and a daughter." His partner looked at him as if he'd lost his marbles and simply played his next shot with no further inquiry.

My coffee was spluttered across the table as I failed to

control my mirth. I was so proud of my husband and the story sounded so funny. I wished I could be as blasé as Richard, yet I knew he was still having an extremely difficult time coping with the changes that Toni was making to her body and to her life.

On 9th January, 1998 Toni and Andrew moved themselves, their business, and their lives to a certain extent, to a rental property. The house they went to was fairly large, had room for a separate office for the business and a large, weather-proof garage where they could set up their work-shop. It would be so much easier for them to carry out their work in the future and we hoped for their success. Their theme song for the business, which they often sang while they worked was – "From little things, big things grow". We all wished this for them.

So they packed everything into a rental truck and moved all their belongings. That is, all except Toni's chihuahua dog P.K. I realise I haven't mentioned P.K. before, so I'll tell you a little about him. He was chucked out of Tony's home in Perth when Tony left, as Judith had given him the dog and she wanted no reminders left behind. So Tony asked could he bring P.K. home as well. Of course we agreed. We already had a dog of our own, Bobo, and Mum's dog, Rex. Another addition to the pets would make little difference – or so we thought!

P.K. was named after the famous mint gum, for some rea-son unbeknown to me and Tony doesn't know why either, but P.K. he was and what a gutsy little dog he was, full of attitude far beyond his size. As there were already two dogs in residence who had long since worked out their territory and position in the household, a newcomer was unwanted. Bobo is placid enough to accept anything, but Rex, well that was a different story altogether. He was top-dog and he did not want any scrawny runt, smaller than your average cat to come into his zone. For quite a while we imagined we would find P.K.'s remains in the garden following one or two confrontations. But can you believe it – P.K. became the new top-dog. He may have been the smallest and newest addition but he soon claimed his supremacy and once that was settled they all became friends. Not quite accurate, Bobo and P.K. were very good mates, but Rex only just managed to tolerate the newcomer.

So when moving day arrived P.K. was left with us, much to Richard's chagrin. Somehow he blamed the poor little fellow for everything that had happened to his son. And I don't think he'll ever forgive the poor dog. Nevertheless he walked him with the two other dogs, fed him and did whatever was necessary for the animals. He just doesn't like P.K. and I don't think he ever will.

Weeks later, when I was out shopping, I came home to discover P.K. had gone. Richard had picked him up, taken him back to Toni and said, "Here, take your dog, he's causing too much trouble with our dogs." He wasn't. But Richard couldn't stand the sight of P.K. I was broken-hearted and couldn't forgive him as I had grown to love the little guy and to me he was all I had left of my former son. We had opposing views about that tiny, innocent chihuahua dog who had become like a pawn in the game of life.

We still saw Toni and Andrew several times a week and whenever Toni came home I heard more and more about the transsexual scene. She needed someone to talk to and Andrew was sick of it all. In fact they had almost come to blows over the subject. Andrew told her to "Shut up about it all or else", and he meant it. Once they had sorted that out between themselves, Toni needed her mother more than ever. Often I wasn't in the mood either, but I didn't have the heart to say so.

A few weeks after they moved, when the summer sales were coming to an end, Toni rang and suggested a day shopping with the 'mother hen'. I liked Raelene, though I had never met her yet. My knowledge of her was from one or two brief telephone calls and from what Toni had told me about her. As I had by then met several other transsexual girls and one boy, I felt I was ready to go out and would be able to cope. I said yes, I would love to go shopping and with just a tiny bit of trepidation we went. I met Raelene and my liking was confirmed. We got on well. Another girl friend was going to join us. Three transsexual women and myself set out for a girls' shopping day and lunch. At first I felt totally at ease and we tried on shoes and looked at clothes. Then we visited a lingerie store. All of the girls bought some underwear, except myself.

The lady at the counter had 'read' them and I began to feel uncomfortable. I understood that was her problem, not mine, and so I tried desperately to disregard the intrusive nagging feelings I was beginning to experience. But I obviously wasn't up to it at that stage.

We lunched together, talked and gossiped and I felt reasonably settled about the situation. If only that one woman had not intruded and caused me to doubt myself. But doubt I did, and the rest of the day was not as comfortable. Nevertheless I noted that I could cope well with how other transsexual girls looked. They weren't my offspring and I felt fine with them. It was really Toni that I thought everyone might stare at. She was mine and I was still struggling to find acceptance. At home it was different and I was comfortable; being out in the public eye was a totally alien situation. I knew how much Toni wished she was not the way she was and I wished it as well.

22

Education

Days had slipped into weeks and I was turning the months on my calendar faster than I thought possible. Toni was well along with her program of visits to one or another of the professionals in the 'team'. Usually she had an appointment with Dr. K… followed shortly after by an appointment with the older psychiatrist Dr. B… The relationship with both doctors was becoming more comfortable for Toni and so it was easier for her, though she was still full of impatient anxiety about whether or not she would be eventually approved for gender reassignment surgery. This was almost the only thing on her mind when her visits became due, though she thought it best not to ask too often and so she attempted to not pester the doctors for any answers.

Whenever she came home from her visit to either of the psychiatrists she attempted to analyse whatever had been said, looking for clues about whether or not she might expect approval. Dr B… was much more forthcoming than Dr K… and fairly soon she began to receive positive feedback and suspected that she would one day be approved for surgery.

All the while Toni was gleaning more and more information about what to expect both from her treatment in the interim and about the eventual operation. She studied everything she could lay her eyes on, both on the internet, and in professional literature, and books written by other transsexuals.

As well as the psychiatric evaluations, there were visits to an endocrinologist, blood tests, X-rays and after a while a visit to Mr. C ... the surgeon. Some time amid all these medical tests a request came to Toni from a research program being conducted at the Monash Medical Centre. So she agreed to become a guinea pig.

The effect that hormones were having on the heart, as opposed to those naturally occurring in genetically born females was one aspect of the research. The scientists wanted to know whether a genetic male taking female hormones would receive the same therapeutic effect as far as lower rates of heart disease was concerned, that generally seemed to be the case among pre-menopausal women.

Toni's cholesterol levels had always been very low, and were still low. Her general health, fitness and body fat measurements were all excellent. The only problem discovered about Toni's health during all the research tests was that she still had iron levels that were a bit low. Her body had not yet recovered from the loss of blood from the castration, although it was now well into the following year. As Toni can't tolerate iron tablets, the doctors simply advised her to eat more red meat. The deficiency wasn't that bad, but Toni was aware of the fact that she must be in perfect health for the time when she expected to undergo further surgery. So she tried to eat more red meat, but couldn't come at the liver in her diet that was also recommended.

When the time arrived for Toni's surgery she would be expected to provide several units of her own blood for transfusion if necessary; a fact that most people would probably be unaware of. Often patients requiring elective surgery choose to store their own blood, but in the case of gender reassignment surgery patients, this was a necessity and not a choice. Of course Toni was anxious that her own blood be as good as she could make it. Whenever she came to visit I made sure red meat was on the menu.

As Toni was learning more and more about her condition, so was I. Much of my education was from living with a transsexual person, from hearing all about studies that were being conducted and listening to anything I could on the subject. Whenever a program was listed in the television guides, word would spread among the community and I heard of several documentaries that would be on television. I watched them all. Uncannily several programs were screened within a few weeks of Toni's return from Perth and we sat glued to the television in an effort to try and understand more about the condition that Toni had.

One of the first documentaries that I viewed was filmed in Europe and was mainly concerning female to male transsexuals. The whole families were interviewed which made the experience especially riveting for me. I remember seeing a young man, who had been born with a female body. He was sitting up in a hospital bed displaying his new male genitals. They looked very real apart from the fact that the colour was somewhat whiter than the rest of the skin on the boy's body. Possibly once his pubic hair had regrown there would be little noticeable difference. His mother was supporting him with approval and admiration. I couldn't help wondering if she felt as good inside as her appearance suggested.

Within weeks of Toni's returning to live with us in Melbourne, she introduced me to a new friend, a young female to male transsexual. He looked absolutely masculine, right down to the beard on his face and his black hairy arms. I simply could not believe that he had been born female. He was an intelligent and very likeable young man and soon we were chatting away very comfortably. I noticed that his main topic of conversation was somewhat similar to Toni's – much about transsexuals and not much about any other subject. However, I was very interested and I mentioned that I wished that parents had a similar support group to T.L.C.

He gave me his mother's telephone number and we arranged a meeting.

Over a couple of cups of coffee I soon discovered that her feelings were very similar to my own and we happily talked about our similar offspring, though we never actually got into any deep and meaningful conversation about our feelings. Maybe if we'd continued to meet we may have been able to open up a little more. She did confide in me that her son used to be a very pretty girl, with curly ringlets. Although she didn't say so, I could tell that she missed her daughter in the same way that I miss my son. We met on a couple of other occasions, but never met alone again, so we didn't continue the relationship. I think my feelings were still too raw at that time and I felt that I would never find the acceptance that she already seemed to have.

I thought that part of the way to acceptance of Toni and her new role in both her life and my own would be through educating myself. Within a couple of weeks I began to study medical literature. A local neighbourhood house held a writing class and I had been going there and writing as a hobby for a while. My tutor had become an occasional confidante, as sometimes I wrote about personal things. Our relationship was always on a teacher, pupil level. Nevertheless she was an understanding and empathetic type of person and when my whole world seemed to be falling apart I confided in her, though briefly, what had happened. She offered to look up some books at LaTrobe University, where she worked. Knowing someone with access to books that I probably would not have been able to find for myself, was a godsend.

A few days later, she arrived at the door of my home laden with books. She warned me that I would be confronted with colour plates of graphic surgery and she wondered if I was ready to see them. If not, she would take those books back. I said that I thought the only way I could face my worst fears was to stare them in the face. So I took all of the books she offered and read them. I confess that I was a bit squeamish and glanced rather quickly at the photographs of the surgery that I expected Toni would one day undergo. Yet I saw enough to know what would happen.

I wasn't quite ready at that time to think too much about surgery; it was what I knew deep in my heart would eventually happen, but I couldn't face it then. First I wanted to know more about Toni's condition.

For the first time I learnt that there was a huge difference between a transsexual person and a transvestite. I discovered that a transsexual is a person with a life-long medical condition. In their book, *True Selves – Understanding Transsexualism for Families, Friends, Coworkers, and Helping Professionals* (Jossey-Bass Publishers, San Francisco, 1996), Mildred L. Brown & Chloe Ann Rounsley describe transsexuals as "individuals who feel they are, or ought to be the opposite sex".

This particular publication has been an invaluable guide and a comfort to me. Its non-judgmental approach and easy to read style was a godsend. After studying a few professional books that I mostly could not understand, I found 'True Selves' became my bible. In conjunction with what I had managed to glean from other sources, the picture was beginning to clear.

My misunderstanding that a transvestite was the same kind of a person as a transsexual was quickly sorted out. I now know that a transvestite is a person, often a male, who likes to cross-dress and mostly does so for some deep-seated emotional or psychological reason, but they do not want to change their body, nor do they believe that they have been born into the wrong sex.

Then there are female impersonators and drag queens, some of whom may also be either transsexuals or transvestites, but not necessarily. They may simply like to perform on stage in that way.

I discovered from 'True Selves' a bit about She-Males, men who are often involved in prostitution and cater for a particular market. Sometimes they have breast augmentation and they dress as women, but they keep their male genitalia intact.

Once I remember my mother-in-law talking about a 'hermaphrodite' – a sort of half man, half woman person. Now I was learning that the new term for that condition is 'intersexed.' These are people born with different chromosomes who may have some male organs and some female, or appear mostly one sex, but are a little of the other as well. This is by no means a medical definition, only my own interpretation of the condition and as I know it is a very complex subject, I am reluctant to say more.

When I went to pick up my copy of 'True Selves', which I had needed to order weeks in advance, I remember how embarrassed that I felt, simply walking into a book shop to collect such a publication. Looking back, I realise how far I have come in my acceptance, not only of Toni, but of all transsexuals and others suffering complaints of a sexual or gender nature.

Early on, when I was first learning about the subject, I thought that Tony would be cured once she had been through a period of psychiatric treatment. I soon found out that the condition is life-long and often life threatening. The rate of suicide among transsexuals is very high. I would not like to put a figure on the statistics or probabilities because I have read so many varying numbers. Suffice to say that I was fearful knowing that these people suffer a great deal, sometimes more than they can deal with.

How could I never have noticed signs of Toni's condition? As I mother, I asked myself the question many times. Yet why should I have been any different to any other person close to him? No one else had ever picked up that he was longing to have a female body – that in fact he actually believed that he was a female, but born into the wrong body.

I discovered in my study of the subject that these people become absolute experts in the art of covering up; they become adept at telling lies and they do anything they can to try and conform to what their birth body is.

When I met a friend of Toni's, a transsexual woman from overseas, who had come to Australia as a student and also to escape from her family in an attempt to live her life in the way she felt she must, she told me a little of her story.

From a young age, her parents were aware that she wished to be female; she always wanted to play with dolls and dress in girls' clothing. This was quite the opposite from Tony. He was always interested in match-box cars and leggo blocks and he had a consuming interest in dinosaurs and other pre-historic animals; all apparently male child pursuits. And he never showed any interest in dressing in female attire. Only recently did I discover that he quite often did cross-dress whenever he could, but he made sure no one ever found out; he was so secretive with this pastime.

Anyway, Toni's friend had no such desire as a child to hide his interests. His parents were distraught and punished him. They did everything they could to try and change him. Once he turned eighteen years old, being from a country where army national service was compulsory, he was sent off to do his stint. His parents were hopeful that this would fix him once and for all. The rigid discipline dished out by army officers only served to convince him that he must escape and follow his dream – to become female. She confided in me about what a terrible time she had in the army and how she had been picked on, as the other young men thought that she was 'queer' and, thinking she was homosexual, treated her as such. To survive, she attached herself to one of the officers, a man who was a homosexual. She acted a role to protect herself and in return the officer repaid the favour and protected her.

When I read 'True Selves' I at last understood that my feelings of shame, fear, hurt, grief, astonishment, guilt and depression were to be expected, but that with time I could learn to overcome these emotions. Some families never get over the shock. I didn't want that to happen to me. I had much to be thankful for in my life and I wanted to be able to survive the body-blow I was suffering.

23

Finding My Way

Acceptance of my son becoming female didn't happen overnight. But the very beginnings of moving forward came only a few days following Tony's return from Perth. I came across a column in *The Age* newspaper, written by Kim Trengove. I thought it must have been directed at me, so close was it to my particular feelings at that time. I underlined one phrase – 'there is suffering, leave it at that.'

The following sentence, which actually referred to a Buddhist philosophy stated, 'acceptance is a lengthy process and noble truths can take a lifetime or two to sink in'. "God, I hope you can help me, I don't think I can wait that long," I silently prayed.

There was no way I could suddenly accept my son as a female, not just then. All through Tony's life, as far as I was concerned, he was a normal male. And my expectations had just been shot to the moon. No longer would he be 'he'. Although he was the father of my grandchildren, what would he be now? He was still the children's parent, but I don't suppose I could refer to him as father any longer, although he was.

Richard and I had enjoyed taking trips to Perth to visit their family home and we always looked forward to those times together as a family with them. I knew it was impossible for that to happen again. I was enduring so many losses. How could I face up to the disappearance of so very many expectations that I had held? I knew I must help myself, but I was very aware that I needed professional guidance to help me on my way.

I read magazines; I looked for self-help publications and basically sought whatever I could to assist my acceptance of the situation I found myself dealing with. A few years previous, a dear friend had mentioned a book by M. Scott Peck titled *The Road Less Travelled*, so I sought a copy.

I found the book at a market and discovered the previous owner had underlined the first sentence in red pen – 'Life is difficult.'

This was an entirely new concept for me to grasp. As I read further, I discovered that this was the first of the Four Noble Truths which Buddha taught – 'Life is suffering'. I realised this was the very same message that I'd found in Kim Trengove's column. Although I have refrained from changing my religion, I figured there was much to be learnt from Buddha.

Suddenly Australia's former Prime Minister, Malcolm Fraser's famous line – 'Life wasn't meant to be easy' – which I thought at the time to be a laughable notion, made sense. Now, I credit him with more than a little common sense and a great deal of psychological knowledge.

Knowing intellectually, that certain things may be true although a new idea for me to grasp, didn't really help a great deal just then. But these printed words sowed a seed in my ravaged mind. The time had come to seek someone to assist me to live what I already had an inkling of.

Prior to Andrew's court case, we had been attending family counselling, at first just Richard and I; then a bit later Andrew came to a few sessions. When the crisis point in our lives happened, we telephoned Maria, our family counsellor, who arranged an emergency session for us. To our surprise, she also had experience working with some transsexual clients. This probably would not have been a surprise to me a bit later on, when I learned a bit more about the problems transsexuals suffer in their lives. Drug addiction is sometimes a side effect of their dilemma. But just then, I was amazed that Maria knew anything at all about these people.

Maria counselled us wisely. She understood that we were all in a fragile state of mind. On the other hand she gave us a few ideas to consider. She pointed out just how much courage Tony had to be able to change his life and do whatever he had to do to live the way he felt he was destined to live – as a woman. I hadn't yet been able to think about his path quite like that, as I was so concerned with my own feelings of loss and grief. At first my main worry was Tony, knowing the distress that he was in, but fairly quickly I was consumed by feeling sorry for myself.

We stopped going to see Maria, mainly because Andrew didn't choose to go any longer, and I felt that we should not take any more of her time with our other personal needs for counselling. This was a family and rehabilitation centre and Maria was overworked as there were so many young people and other families dealing with issues of dependency on drugs and/or alcohol. Somehow it didn't seem fair for us to take any more of her time. Now I realise that a few more visits to her would have been invaluable. She made more sense to me than anyone.

Most of the time, I just kept going, one day at a time. What else is there to do in life anyway? But the truth of the matter is, I hadn't dealt with a lot of stuff that I had to deal with. When I could not stop crying I realised I would definitely need someone else to help me. I think it was around that time that I sought the sleeping pills from the G.P. who had given me such a hard time. At least that old cow sent me searching for another counsellor.

The doctor I'd been seeing as my personal practitioner on and off for a number of years, the one Tony had gone to for a referral to the gender dysphoria clinic, had left general practice to pursue a full-time counselling career. I was aware of her skills in that direction and decided to seek her out to help me.

Unfortunately counselling didn't work out too well with

her. I liked her very much, and I had known her for many years as my G.P. Perhaps that was part of the problem. Maybe I needed someone I'd never met before. However that wasn't the sum total of why the counselling with her wasn't successful.

We began when she started drawing squares and circles on a piece of paper. These shapes represented the family. I was the circle in the centre – or was it the square? The crux of the situation seemed to be that I was the centre pole, with all these people with a range of difficulties around me. And she tried to tell me that none of their problems were my problems. Well I just couldn't see it that way. When you live in a family environment everyone interacts with one another. I understood what she was getting at to an extent. And that's as far as I could follow her illustration.

The next few visits didn't seem to progress much further. I did gain some ground from seeing her. I listened when she said I needed to distance myself from others' problems, and I learnt a few tactics and hints from her in how to get by on a day to day basis. Unfortunately a lot of the time, I just didn't follow what she was on about. Her explanations and guidance didn't gel. And her way of counselling was beyond my understanding. So I stopped going to see her.

For a long time, I relied on other people to listen to me, and that helped. A couple of especially chosen friends, who I realise now were very long-suffering, but what friends are really about, well they listened to my woes and helped me a great deal. They were non-judgemental and open-minded. How lucky I was.

Only now do I realise how much I was stuffing my feelings inside. So much was going on in our household, what with Mum being so ill, the business boring along and Toni popping up from time to time at first, then she began to become Toni full-time. Richard was going through diagnosis of his illness and all of these things meant that I had little time to myself. Sometimes I just wanted to let it all out. If I'd been wiser, I would have found a way to do that, though not in front of everyone. I had no desire to upset the whole family any more than they were. But I needed to let out what was going on inside me. I could have gone out in the car, found a quiet park and had a good howl. Or somehow found some space for myself. These are the things I did not do at that time.

Following the two deaths in our family, I again found I could not cope. Well, that's not entirely the way it was. Yes, I could cope, I had coped, but I seemed to be stuck. Laughter had left my life. I wanted to be able to smile again. I wanted my life to be whole once more. Perhaps I'd never been really whole. I think that everything in life happens for a purpose and I feel blessed to have had such a huge learning curve. 'Life wasn't meant to be easy' after all, and maybe I had to find that out the hard way.

I again sought someone to help me. I found a wonderfully talented young woman to teach me the fundamentals of 'Rational Emotive Therapy'. Along the way I discovered that this young married woman had nursed her mother through a terminal illness and now she cared for her disabled brother who lived with her and her husband. What struck me was how happy she appeared. If she could live happily – then I could as well.

Lauren guided me through several months of therapy. I learnt so much from her. I learnt that I could be happy no matter what happened around me. If one of my sons should die (God forbid) then I could still live and be happy again. There, of course would be a period of grief, but the loss of another person does not exclude future happiness. I'd been so afraid of losing Andrew to his drug and alcohol addiction or Toni or even my husband Richard. Then there was the possibility that my mother's life was drawing to a close. All of these impending losses were looming heavily, though as it turned out none of them have happened. And isn't that just the way it sometimes is? We worry so much about things that never occur. Now I was being shown that even if they did, I could continue, and happily. What a fortunate find Lauren was for me. This was her job, but I felt she was giving so much more than she was paid for. Thanks Lauren. There were a few more difficult times ahead of me and somehow I missed my final two sessions with Lauren. I hope to go back and finish my therapy with her eventually.

When life came washing more dirty water over me, I again was powerless. It was too soon for me to cope with any more. I succumbed to a bout of anxiety and depression. My doctor said I was coping all right. He put me on anti-depressant medication and was going to leave it at that. However I insisted that he refer me to a psychiatrist. By the time the day of my first appointment arrived, I believe I was already over the worst of my illness, but God knows how ill I may have become again if I had not insisted on more professional guidance.

For now I am still seeing this doctor. He has guided me gently to recovery. When I nervously confided in him that I had begun writing a book about this unusual period of my life, I was a bit worried he may say, 'Forget it, put it all behind you and move on with your life.' To me I thought writing my story was moving on. And to my delight he agreed and he said, "You must finish writing your book. Don't let anyone dissuade you. Perhaps as well as helping you, your book will help someone else." I certainly hope so, but for now, it is for me, and as I recall the amazing events of the past two years, I can leave them there where they belong, in the past. But I can remember what a great life experience it has all been and how much I have gained.

I haven't yet learnt to swim and still there are many days when I find I puddle around in the muddy parts of my life. But I have discovered that I can tread water, wait until again the water becomes clear and I found that I can dog-paddle enough to save myself. My life is like that.

24

Where Have All The Flowers Gone?

I noticed that something was wrong with Richard. At first he began to joke about losing his memory or his marbles or both. Being a man, like many others of his generation, he is out of tune with his own body and unwilling to readily admit to any failure it may present. Richard began using his own particular mechanisms to avoid the confrontation that there was indeed a problem.

As well, I was in total denial that my husband might have difficulty with his memory. I constantly reassured him that for a busy executive I didn't think it abnormal to occasionally experience memory lapses and after all he was well into his fifties so I told him – "Your memory may not be as sharp as when you were young, you know darling."

Little things like putting items away in different spots from their usual abode and then forgetting where he'd put them, I did begin to note. But still I thought it was simply a matter of absent-mindedness and told him not to worry. None of this behaviour appeared to me, at first, to be anything particularly out of the ordinary. In fact all through his diagnosis, his symptoms were subtle.

I noticed Richard was becoming stressed. He was having bouts of irrational temper and was using one of his old strategies to avoid thinking about a problem and to distract his mind. He was using extreme 'busyness'. He could not, or would not, relax.

At that time spring began urging me out into the garden; a place you'll rarely find me. I don't enjoy touching soil and so gardening is not my forte. Richard usually does all of the gardening. Nevertheless, the balmy weather had coaxed me into action and I strolled the 'Greenery' to purchase punnets of flower seedlings to line the walk from our front path to the letter-box. I chose marigolds and alyssums; then violas for the cooler shaded areas under the large jacaranda tree. When Richard arrived home from work I eagerly displayed my unusual industry and he praised my handiwork.

So what went wrong when less than a fortnight later the entire row of seedlings which lined the rocks between the path and the rest of our native garden simply disappeared?

"Where have all my flower seedlings gone?" I asked Richard.

"What flowers?"

"The ones I planted last week."

Shamefaced, Richard admitted he must have weeded them out. Although I was very angry, that emotion was almost immediately over-ridden by concern. I began to realise there perhaps was more to Richard's memory lapses than I was prepared to admit and more than could be explained by the stress of his job.

When I confided in my mother she was in more denial than myself and thought the problem lay with me. How could I even suggest there was anything wrong with her son-in-law, he was fine. So once more I tried a period of denial and comforted Richard with platitudes.

Mum and I decided Richard needed a holiday. That would fix him. Duly and dutifully we travelled to New Zealand for a ten day break, a holiday about which Richard now has little recall. Most of the time he slept and I was convinced that Mum was right. He just needed a good rest.

That trip was in late November and I remember it was in

the week prior to Christmas 1996 that Richard's boss of many years and now also our good friend, rang me, knowing that Richard was at that moment travelling home from the office.

"How is Richard?" he asked. I assured him he was well, though still a little tired and that his gastric reflux problem was well treated and he was indeed much better.

"No, I don't mean that Lyn," John said.

Straightaway I knew he had noticed as well. John began to tell me that he was concerned about Richard's health. He had noticed memory loss, lack of the ability to concentrate and something happening out of the ordinary. Richard's secretary had told him of times when Richard had been falling asleep at his desk and other times he had been going to his car in the car-park for a sleep during the day.

I can't explain what a relief it was to have my own concerns finally vindicated. It felt like a warm bath washing away my denial. Now I could openly admit that there was something real happening. John made me promise to keep his call confidential, which I did. That phone call was all I required to release me into taking action.

That evening in bed with Richard, I broached the subject of his health. I put everything to Richard that I had noticed and was as straight and honest as I could be.

"Something seems to be wrong, Richard."

He agreed whole-heartedly and I'm sure he was relieved that I at last believed him. He hadn't been willing to take any steps toward treatment without my urging. But now he was more than ready to seek medical answers.

There was a wait of several weeks to see Professor B..., an excellent neurologist. Weeks became months and test after test was ordered. To begin with standard neurological examinations and tests were completed, then C.T. scans, E.E.G.s and eventually an M.R.I. was done.

I read in the local paper that the Austin Hospital was conducting a research program into memory loss and so I rang the lady in charge. She explained the type of client she was seeking and it seemed Richard might prove a suitable candidate for her study.

Richard's part in the study required him to make himself available for testing over a period of three years. For the first few weeks Richard was subjected to hours of questions and memory tests, some on the computer, some verbal, some involving pictures and objects. An I.Q. test was given at that time and a general physical medical examination was performed by another doctor. I was required to fill out a questionnaire about what I had noticed regarding Richard's memory and there were questions about his general behaviour, etc.

We discovered that Professor B... was closely involved with this particular study, another interesting snippet that linked events around this time in our lives.

At Richard's first consultation, the Professor was non-committal but we thought he was looking for the possibility of epilepsy. When the first tests came back for his perusal they were all quite satisfactory and showed nothing much to assist his diagnosis.

Richard's work was becoming more and more stressful because the company where he'd been employed for more than thirty years was being re-structured. Although Richard never actually feared for his own job, he never quite knew how the new structure might affect him and his peers at work. So everyone began to suggest his problems were caused by work stress and perhaps some of his symptoms had been aggravated by his job. But we both knew his illness had begun long before the re-structure was planned.

Professor B... asked Richard if he was under more than usual stress in his life. Richard told him he was and when the doctor asked him what sort of stress, Richard replied, "Do you really want to know?" He said that he did, it was important to his diagnosis to understand what stress he was living with. So Richard told him our story. Professor B... has a great sense of humour and his reply made us smile.

"Have you got anyone up at Thredbo?" This remark referred to the tragic land-slide that was at that time front-page news. Many people had lost their lives in the skiing village disaster at Thredbo.

During Richard's diagnostic process I had tried to gently inform his mother and his closest brother about Richard's memory difficulties. An incident occurred which made me realise that they must have been struggling with denial.

An attack of asthma had side-lined me and caused me to be absent from a family birthday dinner at a nearby hotel. I insisted to Richard that he attend the party and I would rest at home.

Next day I received two frantic phone calls; one from his mother and another from his brother. "Do you know Richard can't remember that he went with you to Tasmania last month?" they both asked. "Yes, I know." I politely replied, though I could have screamed at them – "What do you think we're spending a fortune on special diagnostic tests for?" I had told them months ago about Richard's problems and I was angry that they should be asking me now if I knew.

Richard and I had spent our thirty-fifth wedding anniversary in Hobart and we had enjoyed a pleasant and romantic long weekend together, though I did notice how much Richard was sleeping. Only following his eventual diagnosis did I realise he had been unwell that weekend and had suffered several seizures.

When Richard had returned from the birthday bash he was quiet and upset.

"What's wrong, Richard?"

"I didn't remember we went to Tassie. How could I forget such a special trip? You know how much our anniversaries mean."

He was angry, mortified that his family had discovered

what he felt to be a shortcoming and he was very distressed and embarrassed about the whole incident. For days afterwards he was depressed

He was fed up with the tests, couldn't cope well at work and didn't know what else he could to do to help himself. Diagnosis was not eventuating. Professor B... as yet was unable to help. Richard asked the doctor whether he would like to speak to John, his boss; perhaps he had noticed something that might be a clue.

That week John happened to ring the Professor because he'd been present when Richard was experiencing an episode which he had for years nicknamed 'weirdies'. Although Richard had explained his symptoms to the doctor they weren't conclusive evidence of what was wrong and the tests failed to confirm what the Professor by now was suspecting – epilepsy. John's telephone call supplied the missing link as he was able to describe in detail exactly what happened when Richard was suffering a 'weirdie'. Immediately Professor B... said, "I know what it is. You have frontal lobe epilepsy." The doctor went on to tell us exactly which part of the brain was being affected and how his particular symptoms as described by John caused certain physical reactions, such as Richard making chewing motions and rubbing his right thumb and fore-finger together.

At last we could put a name to Richard's condition and treatment began. By this time Tony's homecoming and consequent events had also clouded the issue about how much Richard's memory loss was due to stress and how much was due to the epilepsy. Medication still was unable to control the mild seizures.

The next step was to be a consultation with an eminent neuro-psychologist, another Professor in his field. One lengthy visit was all that was required. The Professor completed a several page report and returned it to Professor B... But he told us on the day at the end of the discussions with him that he was convinced that Richard was more stable than most men, that he was coping with stress very, very well. He said he was convinced Richard's memory loss was almost entirely due to his episodes of epilepsy. Of course the stress was probably causing a few more events than usual, as anyone with epilepsy knows they must avoid stress as much as possible – an impossibility given what was happening in our lives.

After much consideration and soul-searching Richard decided he could no longer continue with the type of work he was doing. His doctor agreed and he recommended to Richard's superannuation trustees that he be granted a total and permanent disability payment.

This step required a further visit to the superannuation company's doctor or doctors for confirmation of Professor B...'s diagnosis. Richard and I by then were beginning to feel like frauds. Even some of his work-mates had suggested they couldn't see much wrong with him. If only they were right. Richard loved his job dearly and it was a great loss to him to be forced into early retirement. This wasn't something either of us wanted. After all, I told Richard, "I married you for life, not for lunch."

We arrived at the office of the neurologist working for the insurance company to be greeted with a doctor who was obviously very much in awe of Professor B... and his abilities. After a consultation that lasted less than one hour, he told us that he totally agreed with the Professor and that he would be also recommending that Richard be granted a total and permanent disability retirement package. So from that day onwards I had Richard for lunch as well as for life.

Following quite a long period of adjustment for both of us, which is another story too long to go into right now, we began to enjoy lunch together.

25

Houseguests

As Toni began to be more involved in the transsexual community and with T.L.C., she was beginning to be of support to some of her transsexual friends. I know it helped her to be involved in the struggles of others that were in a similar position to her.

She quite often visited the hospital when other transsexuals were having surgery, particularly those girls who had come from interstate. I should mention that there were one or two female to male transsexuals that she visited as well, but their numbers were much fewer than male to females undergoing surgery; there were simply less of them.

Usually they were alone, with no support apart from T.L.C. and mostly very grateful to have visitors. I was proud of what Toni was doing and knew she was thankful that she was one of the lucky ones as she had support from family as well as from T.L.C.

From time to time someone would need a bed for a while, either prior to a hospital visit, or after, or sometimes they just had nowhere to go. Toni was soft hearted and occasionally provided short term accommodation, though sometimes there were complications and it just didn't work out too well at all.

One such relationship was with a girl she became very fond of. Unfortunately the girl had several problems, one of which was a boyfriend with a drug habit. The girl was quite anorexic and Toni was doing her best to help her sort out her life. Eventually though Toni found she couldn't help at all, and the girl moved to a distant suburb and out of Toni's life. I haven't heard what happened to her after that.

All the while business was slowing down, as Toni's interests were widening. I don't believe her heart was really in her work at that time. There was so much else happening in her head that I think it became difficult to for her to focus on work. Nevertheless, she worked as hard as she could with the orders that kept coming in. It's just that she seemed to stop chasing extra work, and in a small business that could be fatal.

Andrew was finding it difficult to cope with the stream of transsexual visitors to the home and he formed a relationship with a girl from the country. He decided that he would move out of the house that he was sharing with Toni and move to the country to live with his new love. As there wasn't really enough work for two people in the business, this didn't bother Toni too much, so brother and sister parted company for a while.

As seemed to be happening so often in all of our lives, another strange coincidence occurred. A transsexual woman needed somewhere to stay for a while and as Andrew had left there was a spare room. Toni could use help to pay the rent, so she agreed to a meeting with a girl I will call Wilma. Toni sought my approval before deciding on her suitability as a houseguest. I met her and found her to be a likeable person.

Wilma moved in and life went on for a time uneventfully. The more Toni learnt about Wilma's life and her family, the more they suspected how much they had in common. Wilma was married and had two children. She was fighting to be allowed access to them and was suffering a great deal because she hadn't seen them for a long time. Toni could relate to her feelings very well, being in a similar situation.

As they talked more about their past lives they found an amazing link.

When Wilma and Toni were children they had actually met. In fact they discovered that they were related in a distant way by marriage. As I've mentioned, Richard is one of a large family, with several brothers. Wilma was a step-child to one of Richard's sister-in-law's sisters. I have a vague memory of my sister-in-law visiting once, when my children were small and her sister and her children were with her. That must have been the time when Toni and Wilma actually met. Little did they know that their paths were set for a collision course which would occur very much later on in their lives. Wilma remembered quite vividly the house that we lived in and she remembered playing in our lounge room with Tony and his leggo blocks and match-box cars.

While Wilma was staying with Toni, the T.L.C. committee arranged a social dinner and parents or other family members or friends were invited. Meetings were usually for the transsexuals themselves, although I knew there had been one or two exceptions, such as when a husband and wife were intending to stay together and become wife and wife or whatever title you might call the new partnership. At that time there was a couple like this who were attending T.L.C. I thought what a special sort of relationship they must have. They had children and they loved one another and they still wanted to be together. I hoped it would work out for them, and later learnt that they are indeed still together.

Toni invited me to go with her to the dinner that was being held at a café in a trendy Melbourne suburb. I had already met several of the others who would be going and I knew that there would be one mother there whom I had met before, so I said, yes, I would love to go. Richard decided he didn't feel ready to go to a dinner attended by other transsexuals.

By now Toni had stopped wearing a wig and this was the first time she was going out in public au naturel. She had dyed her dark brown hair red and varied the colour often. I told her she would dye her hair to death if she wasn't careful. This period of her transition, Richard unkindly refers to as 'the Frankenfurter period', referring so a slight resemblance to the lead character from 'The Rocky Horror Show'. I think Toni's unease about her appearance served to make me uneasy, as well as increase my nervousness about the evening.

I was seated at a long table next to another mother, who had travelled from a Victorian country town to be at the dinner. She confided that it was the first time she had seen her 'daughter' presenting as a female, either privately or in public. The girl lived with her brother and he had declined the invitation to dinner. He told his mother he had enough of the transsexual scene, living with her on a day to day basis and he didn't feel he wanted to socialise that particular night. So she came alone with her new daughter and she seemed to be very comfortable with her. I, in fact, gained some strength from her composure.

That night, I found it extremely difficult to cope. At first I was fine, but the more I noticed other people walking past our table on the way to the toilet and taking second and third looks, the more uneasy I felt. There were a total of almost thirty transsexuals at our table and two mothers, one brother, a couple of friends and the woman partner that I previously mentioned. If our table had not been on the path to the conveniences, I'm sure everyone would have felt less conspicuous.

Around the time of the dinner and when Toni was doing quite a few hospital visits, she thought it might be a good idea for me to go with her. I agreed. It would allow me time to accustom myself to the fact that Toni's surgery might not be too far into the future. Also, I hate driving through the city and I wanted to know how to get to the hospital as it was on the other side of the city from where I lived.

Toni thought I might be able to cope better when her time came if I knew what the procedures were, what the hospital looked like and what sort of room she would be in, etc. So next time Toni was going visiting I went with her.

It wasn't a case of sticky-nosing or intruding on the privacy of the girls who were in hospital at that time. My visit simply served a dual purpose. One of the girls who had surgery two days previously was from interstate and had travelled alone to Melbourne for her operation. She seemed very pleased to have visitors. Always the patients were asked first if they would like visits from T.L.C. Occasionally a girl who didn't want visits from strangers would decline, and that was fine and we understood.

That day there were three transsexuals in hospital. It was common practice at the hospital for the surgeon to perform surgery on more than one transsexual patient on the same day or within a day or two. Two of the transsexuals that we visited were women and one was a female to male transsexual. I was told he was having his twenty-third (or some similar count, I can't swear to the accuracy of the number) operation.

When a female to male transsexual begins their transformation, there is much more surgery involved, though not normally as many operations as the patient I visited on that particular day.

Often, a female to male transsexual will have a double mastectomy, as breasts are definitely not wanted. A hysterectomy might follow and eventually the patient may seek to have male genitals. This surgery was formerly available only overseas, though I do believe it is now possible to have the operations performed in Australia and by Australian surgeons. The operations are complex and not always totally successful.

What I had noticed, albeit with my own very limited experience, was the fact that female to male transsexuals usually 'pass' very well. Hormone treatment promotes the growth of a beard and bodily hair grows in profusion. A short haircut, some muscle building exercises, combined with the hormones can build a body that easily passes as male. I think if I cut my own hair short, wore a suit and acted in a masculine fashion, it might be possible to pass reasonably well without any extra help from hormones. And I consider myself to be an attractive and feminine sort of woman.

While we were at the hospital I took particular notice of the staff and wanted to see how they treated the transsexuals in their care. I observed that they were not in the least fazed. I knew that they were experienced and they seemed to be a very caring nursing staff. It put my mind at ease once I had been to the hospital and seen the surroundings where Toni would be coming, and I felt much better for seeing the place where my daughter would undergo such drastic surgery.

26

You Wouldn't Read About It

Apart from the fact that Wilma was actually related, albeit distantly and by marriage, a series of coincidences started to string along with our lives. How could so many things occur that seemed meant to be? Many times I have pondered this question and recalled one after another of events occurring in my life's wondrous plan.

After Andrew's court appearance when Richard, Andrew and I went to the hospital, we noticed the beautiful chapel. We did not go in, or really take in what the full wall size stained glass picture illustrated, but I'm sure we all said a silent prayer that Andrew had been granted a reprieve from a jail term. That was the first of three things that came to mean something to us on that particular day.

After visiting Mum, Richard, Andrew and I felt like taking a walk down to Dimmey's, a landmark department type store in Richmond. Often we rummaged around the fascinating shop and picked up a bargain or two. The store was built in 1853 and is so full of charm and character that I don't think there's another like it remaining in Melbourne; at least not still operating as a department store.

Chatting along like the three stooges, we joked and mucked around a bit, full of joie de vivre. I almost tripped on the kerb in our high spirits, when Andrew pointed out an E.H. Holden car that was driving toward us. "Look Mum, an

E.H. just like Tony's." Sure enough, same two-tone grey and white, equivalent sort of condition, Holden car drove past us. The driver was a tall man with dark hair. At that moment it just seemed like a happy reminder of our loved one so far away and we made no further mention of it.

A few minutes later we were wandering around our favourite old store, not really shopping but just glad to be doing a normal family thing together free of any concerns. Then we were jolted back to Perth with a loud call over the store's inter-com system. "Tony Langley, telephone call, Line 1, back store-room. Tony Langley, telephone call, Line 1." Richard, Andrew and I looked at one another, surprised that someone working at Dimmey's had the same name as our Tony, and even more surprised that we'd been again reminded of him in a matter of less than half an hour.

This time we did comment further on what a coincidence it was that we should have seen 'Tony's car' then hear his name called. Even so we were unaware of how much these two incidents would come to mean to us. We spent a few minutes talking about Tony, wondering how much more he'd been able to restore his old car, and generally chatted about how he might be getting on. Our peaceful outing was not disturbed by the knowledge of what must have been really occurring in Perth at that very time. (Probably this was almost exactly when Tony was performing 'surgery' on himself.)

My inner concerns about Tony during that fateful shopping expedition were stirred when we heard Tony's name called. I had spoken to Tony by telephone a few days earlier and distance could not hide his distress. Only a couple of weeks earlier Tony had confided in me that he had something he had to tell me. I knew by the tone of his voice that this wasn't going to be pleasant news.

"Are you gay?" I asked, though God knows why. To this day I don't know why I even voiced such a suggestion. I never, ever thought that, and I still don't. Tony is not gay. I would not care if he were. But no, that wasn't it. Something must have led me to realise this problem Tony was trying so hard to divulge had something to do with a deeply personal, possibly sexual, nature. That wasn't it either. Actually it turned out to be nothing to do with sex, but at that time I probably thought gender-related difficulties were sexual. Now I know they are not at all.

"I want to be a woman," Tony blurted out. Well, I was so stunned and shocked that I cannot remember what I thought. I think that I was concerned for Tony's state of mind more than anything else as I could tell he was depressed and I knew his marriage was in serious trouble.

I kept that phone call to myself for more than a little while. How could I tell Richard? I remember I was a bitch to live with during that time, so confused and upset was I within my own mind, with no ability to share what was happening. Tony had asked me to keep his confidence. He would tell his father himself, when he found the courage. I talked to him and begged him to seek psychiatric help, which he did.

27

Providence

From that day when I learnt for the first time what Tony was going through and had suggested he see a doctor, many more meetings with people, who seem now to have been part of a pre-ordained plan for us all, began to be set in motion.

On that first sad and dark winter evening when we met with a family counsellor with Andrew, our eyes began to be opened. The blinkers were being removed. We discovered a great deal about transsexuals during that session with Maria. She told us much that she had learnt in her dealings counselling those people. She said they were a group of the most courageous human beings she had ever dealt with. "Their problems are life-long," she said. And I had thought once Tony moved back to Melbourne, he would begin treatment with a psychiatrist and all would be well again.

Maria described some of the types of behaviour we might expect both from Toni and from others that she would almost certainly befriend. That idea had not begun to occur to me. But Maria assured us that Toni would want to mix with people in her own peer group where she would feel comfortable. At first they would test her and she would endure a sort of probationary initiation period before she would be fully accepted as one of them. "Transsexuals can be very bitchy," she told us.

As I reflect on the people who were at that time part of

our life and who happened to be experienced with the transsexual community, I cannot fail to be totally amazed. It seemed all so pre-set for us.

Andrew had a further appointment with the doctor at Moreland Hall, a drug and alcohol rehabilitation clinic. This was a week or two following his return from Perth with Tony. Dr. J... had been contacted while Andrew was interstate as he needed to know why Andrew had missed an appointment. It was important that there be a genuine reason as visits to the doctor were part of his bond.

When Andrew came home from his visit to see Dr. J... he couldn't wait to tell us his particular piece of news. Dr. J...'s good friend is the surgeon performing gender re-assignment surgery at the hospital where Toni ultimately would have her operation. The doctor had discussed what had happened to Tony in Perth with his friend and joked to Andrew about it. The surgeon had told Dr. J... and he in turn told Andrew what he'd said – 'What does he think he's doing, trying to put me out of business? I can do the operation for him.'

Then there was my G.P. whom I've already said was at one of the first 'sex-change' operations in Melbourne, so she also had quite a bit to offer me in both information and support in the situation our family was now living.

Coincidence followed coincidence, never failing to astound me. Like when Toni first began her hormone treatment and she was so worried about presenting a prescription to a pharmacy. She was afraid she would be questioned as to the reason, or looked at in a funny way and then she would feel embarrassed. Anyway she nervously presented her script at the local pharmacy next door to the surgery where my G.P. worked and discovered the young woman there to be very kind and friendly. It wasn't long before she knew Toni's story, partly from myself and partly from Toni. We soon learnt that her own special masseur who she used for relaxation therapy was a transsexual woman, so she felt totally comfortable with the subject.

Over the period of the transition of Tony to Toni, one by one more and more of these peculiar incidents began to infiltrate our family. Just when we needed someone, they popped up like magic in our story. If I didn't know it was all fact, I wouldn't believe it all myself, so amazing does it seem to me in reflecting back.

How come Paul's dentist happened to be there for him on the very day of Toni's surgery? – a story I'll tell you about later. Then of course, there was the social worker at Epworth who was so kind and knowledgeable. You could be forgiven for thinking that all professional medical people have experience or knowledge in the field of transsexualism. But they don't. There are actually, in number per population a tiny percentage of transsexuals and even some doctors have little knowledge about the subject, so the odds of us stumbling upon so many people who would be able to help, is staggering. I don't expect I'll ever win Tattslotto. I figure I've used up my share of good luck in finding so many people to help me when I needed them most.

As I previously mentioned, my writing tutor was aware of my story at the very beginning. I knew what a broad-minded person she was so immediately she was one of the few people I confided in. Her assistance was invaluable. Although she didn't have personal experience or knowledge of the subject, her suggestion was that education was the best way to deal with something unknown and that I may feel less threatened and frightened if I have as much education as possible. That was when she arrived at my home laden with an armful of books. She had warned me that I would be confronted with colour photographs of surgery and should be prepared to face them. So began my education in something about which I had only read blurbs in sensational pages of women's magazines and trashy type journals.

28

All Sorts of News

Our second Christmas with Toni as our daughter had come and gone. We'd spent a quiet time at home with the family, following our former traditions. The day was spent devouring hot food and opening heaps of gifts.

On New Year's Eve Richard and I went to a small party with friends and relatives while Mum was in the care of my cousin who often took turns in looking after her, for which I am eternally grateful. We put our cares aside for the evening and welcomed 1999 with great hope for our family.

By 2 a.m. we had slipped into a peaceful sleep, dreaming of happier times, only to be awoken by a telephone call at 4 a.m. My mother had fallen while getting up to the toilet. She had broken her hip and was in an ambulance on the way to hospital.

The emergency ward doctor spoke to Richard and I privately, informing us that the chances of Mum surviving the surgery, considering her serious lung condition and overall state of health were extremely poor. My negative attitudes came to the fore and I had her dead and buried. I should have known better. My mother is made of tough stuff. She was determined to hang around for me a bit longer, perhaps to see us through the still challenging time of Toni's surgery.

Over the Christmas period, Toni was awaiting her own longed for gift – the okay from the team. She knew that they were meeting before Christmas, but her next appointment wasn't until February. This was a particularly stressful period for Toni. Several times she said to me that if she wasn't approved, she would suicide. I told her I didn't want to hear any more of that kind of talk. It was too upsetting for me. If that was her decision, then I didn't want to know about it. I suggested that she try and be patient. She had already waited a long time to fulfil her dream of becoming a woman, but after all, it was only eighteen months since she began her transition. How real her suicidal intentions were and how much was attention seeking, I wasn't prepared to gamble on. I hoped that Toni would soon hear good news and then we would all be put out of our miserable wait. It had been a long time for her family as well as for herself.

Toni heard that two transsexuals had suicided. My fears were again aroused, as I understood how extremely hard life was for many transsexuals. Christmas and New Year had obviously proven too painful for two of Toni's friends.

However, Toni did not dwell on the sad news; she was so anxious to hear what her own fate would be. The team had conferences every now and again, I wasn't privy to the exact workings of their program, but I had heard that Toni's case would be discussed at their next meeting. All of the doctors who had seen her had prepared reports, I gather, and they would be assessed to help decide whether she would be approved for surgery. Toni would not know until she had her next appointment with Dr. K... in early February.

At last the day arrived and joy, joy, joy, she had been approved.

Dr. K... had asked Toni how soon she would be prepared to go into hospital. They had a date in mind – the next month. Toni's happiness was somewhat short-lived as her private hospital insurance would not be available to cover her until April. So she told Dr. K... she was unable to accept that date. The next available time that the surgeon could offer was not until August. So a date was set. Toni's gender re-assignment surgery would be performed at a hospital in Melbourne on 17th August, 1999.

I was relieved to have time to adjust to the prospect of Toni's major surgery. There were risks involved, I knew that much, and so once again I turned to a little study of the subject of the surgery in an attempt to face my fears. I forced myself to look at illustrations of what would happen when she went under the knife.

Penile inversion would be used to create a vagina. This involved using only the skin of the penis. I had learned that the tip of the penis is conserved to create a clitoris because of the sensitivity of that area. Usually an orchidectomy, or removal of the testicles is carried out. This, of course, was not necessary in Toni's case, as that had already been done. Toni still had the skin of the scrotum area and I think the surgeon uses some of that skin as well. As I have no medical knowledge, these facts are what formed an outline of what I thought would occur during surgery. I can't say how entirely accurate my ideas about the surgery are, but I think this is roughly what would happen.

The other major part of the operation was to re-arrange 'the plumbing'. I was very concerned about this part of the operation. Toni had had a bit of trouble with one of her kidneys a few years earlier and I was fairly sure she had neglected to inform the surgeon as she would have been afraid that her chances of being selected for surgery might be compromised.

Prior to surgery Toni was required to have more blood tests, to make sure she had no serious infections or viruses. She must then begin to store her own blood in preparation for surgery. Apart from the medical side of things, Toni needed to get her house in order as far as the business was concerned.

She decided she would do as much work as she could prior to surgery, and stagger her workload so that she had a quiet period around August. She didn't want to tell any of her customers that she would not be available, for fear of them sending work to her competition. Her intention was to stall any orders, complete what she could and to tell her clients that she had a full book and they would need to wait a little longer than usual for their orders. Hopefully that would work out for her.

Mentally, we all needed to prepare ourselves for Toni's surgery. I thought that I had come a long way in my acceptance of her new role, but I also suspected that I would come up against emotions that would be difficult to cope with when the time actually arrived.

There were other practicalities that needed attention. I had given Toni a new nightie and dressing gown, hoping that she would keep them for hospital. But she was so pleased with them she had worn them a lot and she had no other night attire for her hospitalisation. She needed to shop for nighties and pack a bag in readiness. It seemed to me something like the time when I was preparing for Tony's birth. This time in a way it was another birth, the birth of my daughter, Toni.

29

A Holiday, Hope and Hospitals

A short cruise on the majestic liner QE2 provided Richard and I with much needed respite that would prove more beneficial than we could have known. Yet more challenges lay ahead for us.

Richard was retired now and we'd been through an extremely stressful period in our lives. The holiday worked wonders. We were ready to make plans for our future. We held hopes that life would progress more smoothly now for our family, in preparation for the time when Toni's gender re-assignment surgery was scheduled.

Part of Richard's superannuation package was earmarked for a dream home. This was high on our wish list. Our present abode was ageing, and none too gracefully. It wouldn't be long before major renovations were required. At the very least quite a bit of maintenance was required so it made sense to consider moving to a newer, grander home.

My own goal was not only for a new home but also to make a fresh start. I knew that I could not run away from the recent past yet I felt a new home might help provide a symbolic new beginning in which we could all move forward with our lives.

Autumn days quickly dropped more than colourful leaves on to our laps. The changeable weather encouraged a few bugs and viruses. Richard succumbed; he began to feel ill and had a hacking cough. A visit to his G.P. reassured him that a seasonal virus was probably attacking him, but that he should feel much better in a day or two. No treatment was required.

Richard's cough did not deter him from house hunting with me. We had been looking around for a few weeks at that time and had almost decided to forget the idea for a while. Nevertheless we went out again and soon actually signed a contract to buy a large contemporary style home.

The front of the house and the entrance looked tranquil. I think the serene appearance from the outside was what first attracted us to inspect further. A slate path wound up to a wide glass front door. As we walked inside we knew we had found our dream home. It was larger than we required but we decided we could live with some extra space. Everything else about the home was just lovely. The only drawback that concerned us was the fact that the home was built on several levels and we were a bit worried whether Mum would be able to cope with the steps. Nevertheless we purchased the home.

That night my sleep was disturbed by Richard's continual cough and he was beginning to have drenching sweats. I suggested that he make another appointment for a consultation with his G.P., but he was determined that he would be better soon.

My concern over Richard's health was put to one side when we received news of the death of Richard's cousin's twenty-one year old son. He had suffered a severe asthma attack that proved fatal. Sadly, another young person among our extended family had died.

So determined was Richard to attend the funeral that he delayed treatment of his now worsening 'virus'. On the morning of the funeral day, Richard attended his doctor, expecting some antibiotics and a quick cure. But he ordered X-Rays and blood tests. Still Richard insisted on being present at the funeral, so between tests we attended, with his X-Rays left outside in the car. Richard sat and shivered throughout the service. His face was in turn scarlet, then deathly white between sweats. As soon as the service was over I rushed him back to his G.P. who immediately organised a bed in a private hospital. The doctor diagnosed bi-lateral pneumonia. Within two hours, Richard was tucked between sterile white sheets.

A thoracic specialist gave an encouraging prognosis, suggesting that two or three days intravenous antibiotic treatment and bed rest should be sufficient and he would be well on the way to recovery. But Richard only got sicker. His liver had stopped functioning and signs were that his condition was deteriorating. He was indeed very ill. This pneumonia was different and not responding well to the antibiotics. Legionnaire's Disease was a prime suspect.

Toni arrived at the hospital to visit her father, full of both concern and elation. She was worried about her dad's condition but couldn't conceal her delight in her own news. There had been a cancellation. Mr. C... the surgeon could now operate on Toni on 12th June, only five weeks away.

While Richard was in hospital our home was on the market, so between visits, I was caring for Mum, cleaning house and doing the 'fresh flower bit' to tempt prospective purchasers. Each day I prepared the house in readiness for the estate agent to bring clients, before rushing to Richard's bedside.

Now I had Toni's news to masticate. It was too soon. 'Oh no, I can't cope,' I thought. 'Not yet, please dear God, not yet. You said August. I thought I still had more time to adjust.' But my silent bargaining pleas fell on deaf ears.

Meanwhile my mother's health was again precarious. She was wheezing more and had begun to cough more than usual. The changeable late autumn weather was affecting her asthma quite badly.

Between hospital visits, house cleaning and caring for Mum, I found the timing of Toni's surgery mind boggling. I began to suffer anxiety. Each day I prayed for the strength to complete my tasks with my mind still intact. I think a certain amount of denial about the seriousness of Richard's condition helped me, coupled with the doctor's optimism that he would pull him through. Somehow I managed to maintain a measure of sanity.

Nine days later, Richard was discharged from hospital, still quite ill but recovering. Unfortunately by then Mum was getting sicker and two evenings later I once again took her to hospital. For some reason that I can't recall I didn't call an ambulance. I must have thought she wasn't quite that ill. But she was. Again she was admitted to Epworth Hospital.

Now I had Richard convalescing at home, house cleaning each day in preparation for estate agent visits plus hospital visiting to Mum. I'm not saying, 'Oh, poor me,' but it was simply more than I could handle all at the one time.

And Toni's surgery was looming closer every day. I was trying to get my mind into order as well as my house. I knew that Toni would need me, but I felt the pressure of time against me. Somehow I must find the power to cope within myself.

So, whenever I could I found a few spare minutes. I took time-out. I read a book, took long, soaking lavender baths, bought a new outfit, shopped for some night attire for Toni to wear in hospital and I read whatever motivational, inspirational stuff I could lay my hands on. And I drank a glass of wine with my evening meal.

I was well aware there were occasional failures in gender re-assignment surgery though I tried not to dwell on negatives. The techniques employed by surgeons were well advanced, so the risks were less than ever. I refused to contemplate any complications and I prayed that Toni would be transformed to the way that she felt she must be and that she would make a total and speedy recovery. I also prayed for my own acceptance of her in her new body.

30

G-DAY (Gender Re-assignment Surgery)

A privet hedge partially conceals the small private hospital from the view of the bustling, predominantly Jewish community who reside in the area. The humour and the irony of the fact that the hospital is basically Jewish, though open to all, does not escape my wandering mind. Isn't gender re-assignment surgery for a Male to Female, taking circumcision a bit too far? I decided not to confide my wicked and warped sense of humour to Toni as this was hardly the time or place. Tomorrow would be 12th June, 1999 and the beginning of a new life, both for Toni and for myself.

We arrive early at 3.10 p.m. Toni was to be at the hospital at 4.00 p.m. Nevertheless the receptionist is not bothered. She asks us to wait and Toni will be admitted to her ward.

While we're waiting in the reception area, Stephanie, a young friend of Toni's arrives. I feel annoyed. This is my time with Toni. I also face my prejudices once again. I had never met Stephanie before but I knew she was a 'working girl'. Never having met a prostitute before, I held no pre-conceived ideas of what she might look like, but plenty of judgmental attitude to deal with.

Carol, a kindly professional nurse, shows us to Toni's room. Stephanie buys magazines for Toni and promptly plonks herself down in a chair in the room as Toni is taken through the necessary paper work. I still think Stephanie is intruding. I know she had her 'operation' about a year ago and that Toni was very kind to her. Stephanie has not forgotten.

As soon as Carol completes the formalities, Stephanie jumps up and fusses around making us both a cup of tea and biscuits. She asks my star sign and when I tell her it's Cancer, she tells me she likes those people, they're warm, home-loving and generally soft-hearted people. I begin to warm to Stephanie. This is a difficult day for all of us and the girl's kindness is genuine. I feel sorry that I pre-judged her so much, and am actually glad that she has come.

The first thing I noticed about Stephanie's appearance is that there was really nothing to notice. She looked so ordinary, your typical girl next door kind of young woman. Apart from her large breasts, but then many small women have large breasts. Because I knew that Stephanie is trans-gendered I guessed that she had probably had a breast augmentation 'job'. Toni later confirmed this was so.

My emotions were strained, as they had been for the last week. I had been thinking about how far I had come in my acceptance of Toni and the whole situation that our family was in, and I knew I would probably find some emotions that were unexpected when the day arrived. I did. But I actually didn't take time to analyse what I was feeling; I think a range of conflicting emotions. The concern of Toni entering such a major surgery was certainly one thing that had entered my mind. As a mother, that was my first consideration. Then I was wondering how the males in our family would be feeling.

Stephanie expressed it very well, when she asked about Toni's siblings. When Toni told her she had two brothers, she asked how they were feeling and put the issue in words I had not thought of – 'A paradoxical irony. Their nightmare is our dream'. That's it exactly, Stephanie. A transsexual male to female cannot wait to be rid of their male genitalia. Toni's brothers could not imagine anything worse.

Sometime between 8.05 a.m and 12.15 p.m. on 12th June, 1999, Toni's body was transformed as much as the skill of a scalpel and human hand and brain can achieve, to that which, hopefully will be undetectable from the genitalia of a genetically born woman.

I rang the hospital High Dependency Unit, where I knew Toni would be spending about 24 hours. It was 12 noon. Toni wasn't back yet. My stomach was churning, though I wasn't overly concerned because I knew the surgery took about four to five hours. Ring again in an hour, I was told.

Paul rang during this time with a story that astounded me with its coincidence and timing. The irony of so many happenings never fails to strike home. He had an appointment with his dentist that morning, and was joking about being just as scared as probably Toni is, that I doubted, and I guessed Paul didn't mean it either. During his dental visit, he began chatting. The dentist also does body and ear-piercing. I knew that, as my daughter-in-law used to be his nurse before my grandchildren were born. The girls had their ears pierced by him. Mary wouldn't take them to any other dentist because she knows Dr. S…'s high standards as far as sterilisation and cleanliness. Anyway, Dr. S… told Paul about the boob-piercing job he had just finished for a patient, complete with a chain from one breast to the other. "Bizarre" he commented.

"Not as bizarre as what my brother is having done this morning" Paul told Dr. S… "Oh? Is he having a sex-change?"

Paul told me he nearly fell off the chair with surprise that Dr. S… had guessed so easily, and the ho-hum type of expression the dentist used. "My brother/sister had a sex-change fifteen years ago," he offered in explanation.

Paul then had the opportunity to discuss with another man their similar situation as brothers of an M to F transsexual. Now what kind of fate brought two people together like this on the very morning of Toni's surgery, actually while Toni was in the operating theatre? Something or someone was working to ease things for our family, no doubt about it. Paul had been having a difficult time trying to find some acceptance of the situation. He just didn't understand.

When I arrived with Richard to visit the High Dependency Unit we were both scared. We didn't know quite what to expect. Toni was the only patient in the room although there was another bed. Later in the day, or perhaps the following morning another transsexual woman would occupy the empty bed. I was wondering how I would feel with another person and possibly their family around them. I just felt that I needed to be alone with Toni at that particular time. The situation was too difficult to deal with to have strangers in the room with us.

Toni was lying on her back with her legs apart and she was connected to a drip. Her face had a waxen appearance, her skin almost translucent. A film of perspiration had formed on her brow and her top lip. She was in a lot of pain and asked for more relief. The nurse, seated at a small desk only a metre away, could only offer some Panadeine as it was not yet time for her stronger dose of analgesic. No matter how much pain my daughter was in, she was very concerned about her appearance and wanted to know about how her hair looked. It actually looked dull and lifeless and naturally enough, following a major operation, she was no oil painting. Yet I assured Toni she looked just fine. I smoothed her dark locks, her own natural hair was long now and she pushed my hand away, upset that her receding hairline may become noticeable. Her mood was aggravated by the amount of pain she was suffering and I could not console her. We stayed an hour or so, then told her she must rest. I promised to return the following morning. Toni hoped to be moved out of High Dependency into her own room again. I felt the need for more privacy and hoped so too.

By the time I visited it was early afternoon, as Toni had rung and said not to come until she had moved out of High Dependency and she was still there in the morning. Back in her room, Toni seemed to be somewhat irrational. I was beginning to be concerned about her state of mind. Her mood was all over the place and I was worried. When I left the hospital I wasn't sure whether to contact her psychiatrist or what to do. She was being cared for by a most professional group of nursing staff. So I decided surely they would notice something was amiss and do whatever was necessary.

However, next day her moods were even more erratic. I suggested to Toni that her psychiatrist be contacted. She was adamant that Dr. K... should not be called. The nurses had said the high doses of pain killing drugs had probably caused her distress. Also the nature of the operation causes a high degree of physical and mental adjustment. I wondered when my daughter would return to a more normal state of mind. I couldn't stand seeing her the way she was. I cut my visits as short as I could reasonably do so. Toni needed me there, but she also had lots of other visitors, perhaps too many. Maybe that was part of the problem.

As soon as Toni could get up and walk around a little she began to improve. Her natural inquisitiveness helped her. Soon she was walking around the corridors, visiting the other girl and chatting to a few other patients. She told me she even wandered down to the nursery to visit the maternity ward babies. Toni began to recover both mentally and physically. I was so relieved as I had begun to think she was totally losing the plot.

After seven days a second minor operation was performed, which was the way we had been told the procedure worked. This completed the physical transformation and hopefully no further surgery would be required, although there was always the possibility that if there was insufficient length in the vagina that had been created, some time in the future there may be the need for another visit to hospital.

Toni went to the operating theatre and was back in her room in a couple of hours. Soon she was up and around once more and she hoped within three days she would be discharged.

This was the ultimate dream for my daughter. Her body now matched her inner conception of how she should look. Transition was now complete – but really this was just the beginning. Life would continue to offer challenges for her to overcome. Her condition is life-long and not suddenly 'cured' by gender re-assignment surgery. But for now she was ecstatic that her body was much closer to the way she felt it ought to be.

Over the relatively short period of twenty-three months, Toni had achieved an amazing transformation in her appearance. At the beginning of her transition when she wore heavy make-up, a wig and sometimes overly feminine garb until today, the day of her discharge, she had blossomed from a chrysalis to a butterfly.

When I picked up Toni to bring her home she wore her dark hair to shoulder length, fringed across her forehead. Her make-up was light and skilfully applied in shades that complemented her dark features. She wore a simple white T-shirt, black stretchy trousers and a pale grey cardigan.

Although she was a bit too thin, this added to the elegance of her tall frame and by then she had learned to walk like a woman. I noticed, with perhaps a hint of bias, that she is a very beautiful woman. She was still a little pale, as one would expect following such a major operation, but nevertheless she looked quite lovely. I realised as we walked to the car how very far I had progressed in my acceptance of her.

'After all,' I thought with pride, 'She's my daughter.'